Southern Hospitality, Texas Style

Beverly Crowson Gentry

Editor: Dan Lobb

Southern Hospitality, Texas Style
Copyright © 2019 by Beverly Crowson Gentry

All rights reserved. No part of this book may be reproduced or transmitted in any form or by any means without written permission from the author.

ISBN 978-1-7347936-0-5

Printed in USA by

Dedication

To my husband Byron, my partner for life; and my children Max and Raychal; and my lovely grandchildren for whom I consider these delicious family recipes to be demonstrations of love.

This cookbook is also dedicated to the fearless pioneers and founding families of the great state of Texas, their descendants, and all who live today continuing to promote the culture, values and traditions found in the Lone Star State.

Table of Contents

Introduction

Chapter 1 – A Little Texas Culinary History 1

Chapter 2 – A Little Texas Family History 7

Chapter 3 – Let's Get Started 18

Chapter 4 – Bread and Breakfast 51

Chapter 5 – The Main Event 105

Chapter 6 – On the Side 145

Chapter 7 – Perfect Endings 171

Chapter 8 – This and That 211

Chapter 9 – Setting Up Your Kitchen.................... 227

Chapter 10 – Meal Preparation 237

Recipe Index 243

Introduction

After many years of taking culinary, baking and pastry courses (I am a baker, my husband the better cook, and neither of us claim to be a chef), collecting family recipes, including those handed down through many generations, as well as inheriting a small cookbook collection that I've expanded to over five hundred and eighty volumes, multiple recipe boxes, and endless notebooks filled with recipes for almost any dish imagined. I decided to gather a compilation of my interpretations of my favorite Texas dishes to share with my children and yours.

Feeding family and friends, whether casually having a cookout or preparing a sit-down dinner, is the cornerstone of the Southern lifestyle. A Southern woman will feed you when there is a birth, death or any stages in between. You will NEVER enter a southern household where you aren't offered at least cake/pie, or a cookie and a glass of sweet iced tea or steaming coffee. To us, food is love and we share it with pride. The best recipes are those that have been handed down through the generations and are somewhat easy to make with fresh ingredients and just a touch of love.

While many cookbooks include how to set up a kitchen, with weights/measurements, and substitutions I thought it might be fun to spend some time sharing knowledge about the culinary history of Texas as well as some of the more colorful stories about a couple of the founding families: the Parkers and the Crowsons.

Understanding the many influences on Texas cuisine will help you to understand the culture which is the first step to really enjoying some of the traditions and specialty foods that Texans love. I promise that if you are already a Texan, you will be amused by stories you will immediately relate to and if you aren't already a Texan, by the time you finish reading, you will have the dawn of understanding and hopefully enjoy some very special recipes.

Additional Resources

There was not enough space to include photos of all the recipes and techniques covered in this book. These can be found on my blog, Instagram, and Pinterest listed below:

https://www.SouthernHospitalityTexasStyle.com

https://www.instagram.com/Gentry5684/

https://pinterest.com/912WMain

Big Tex from Texas State Fair

Chapter One
Texas Culinary History

For many Texans, a trip to Six Flags over Texas amusement park, in Arlington, Texas was an annual pilgrimage to open the Summer season. Kids of all ages walked into the front gates where the Six Flags over Texas were proudly displayed. Riding roller coasters, eating pink things (creamy pink popsicle), and seeing a musical show were just a few of the activities enjoyed by so many. Spending a day at Six Flags was and still is almost every Texas child's wish for amusement in the heat of summer.

What many don't realize, from a culinary perspective, is that the six flags displayed at the entry gate signified the influence of various cultures in the development of our state and the impact on Texas cuisine today.

Six Flags over Texas:

Spain, 1519-1685 and 1690-1821
France, 1685-1690
Mexico, 1821-1836
Republic of Texas – German influence, 1830-1850
Confederacy, 1860-1870 (although the Southern influence actually began in the 1830's due to the many southerners migrating to Texas)
Modern, representing the United States (U.S.)

Spain

The Spanish influence in what is now known as Texas was prominent in two distinct timelines: 1519-1685 and 1690-1821. The Spanish brought ranching and livestock such as cattle horses, mules, and burros as well as sheep, goats and swine. Most of the processes and procedures surrounding livestock were learned from the Spanish.

France

While the French explorer La Salle led an expedition into Texas and a settlement was established at Matagorda Bay in 1685, the settlement failed. The French continued to claim Texas until the Louisiana Purchase, but the French influence on Texas cuisine came about later.

In the 19th and 20th centuries with the migration of people from Louisiana and some directly from France. French Texans contributed to the growth of Texas by adding business, culture and education.

Cajun and Creole dishes were introduced to Southeastern Texas with this migration. An enduring tradition is "a boil" (crawfish boil, shrimp boil, and crab boil) was prepared in large boiling pots and shared with family, friends and neighbors. Seafood shacks could be found from Galveston to Padre Island where they served gumbo and blackened fish. Creole food reflected French, Portuguese, Spanish, German, and African traditions. Cajun cuisine is a more rustic style imported with Acadian French deported by the British from Canada to Louisiana, and some migrated to Southeast Texas.

Mexico

Probably the greatest food influence came from Mexico. Texas is known for Chili Con Carne. Texas chili is made with beef, whether hamburger, sirloin, or tenderloin, but NEVER contain beans.

Many accounts reflect Tex-Mex was created in the Rio Grande valley as it was an area close to Mexico so there was a large population of Mexicans working on cattle ranches on the border and into the Texas regions. Fajitas, tacos el carbon were introduced on the range.

The first mention of the term Tex-Mex was introduced in 1875 but was not popular until the establishment of the Texas Mexican Railway in the 1920's. The term was used to describe people of Mexican descent born in Texas and it was much later that it was used to describe food in the area.

Although the food had gained some recognition in the Rio Grande Valley, it truly became popular in San Antonio. In the 1870's women in the industrial areas as well as the center of city made chili as it was a fast and flavorful way to feed the many businesspeople and workers in the area. "Chili Queens" set up tables, small fire pits and hung large crocks and pots where they stirred their individual chili recipes to feed the masses.

The "Chili Queens" had international fame with visitors to the area always flocking to the City center to stroll between the tables and consume a hearty bowl of red. Often the ladies set up in the plazas of San Antonio and could have been considered Texas's first pop up restaurants.

In the early 1900's, a man name Otis Farnsworth created the combo plate that typically consisted of beans, rice and an entrée. The first chain restaurants came to Dallas in the 1930's; El Chico and El Fenix. Another invention, the Frito chips, also in the 1930's were created by a Oaxacan immigrant who sold the idea to Elmer Doolin at Frito Lay, based in San Antonio. Soon, the chili pie was born!

Another lovely addition to Tex-Mex cuisine came from Ignacio "Nacho" Anaya who came up with Nachos in the 1950's. When some military housewives came to his restaurant in Piedras Negras, Mexico, finding the cook unavailable Ignacio put together tortilla chips, cheese and jalapeno peppers and placed them under the broiler to melt the cheese. The ladies really enjoyed the dish and soon there were daily requests, so he decided to update his menu to include the tasty dish.

Republic of Texas – German influence

From 1836 to 1845, Texas was its own country. There were quite a few people from German descent that ended up in what we now have termed the "Hill Country".

In central Texas and the Hill Country, the primary influence was from Germans who immigrated to Texas and brought with them the love of smoked meats and sausages. Although these areas are known for breakfast tacos (Austin) and food trucks, the roots of chicken fried steak and barbecue can be traced back to the Germans who settled in the central Texas and Texas Hill Country.

Confederacy – Southern Influence

A brief sixteen years after joining the U.S. as the 28th state, it seceded to join the confederacy.

The Texas tradition of Southern style cuisine dated back to the 1830's. There were many who immigrated from the plantation states, including Tennessee, West Virginia, and Mississippi.

Dishes such as fried chicken, chicken fried steak, peas (cream, purple hull, or black eyes), greens (collard, mustard, turnip or poke salad), mashed potatoes, cornbread or corn pone, sweet tea and desserts (some cakes but more emphasis was placed on cobblers and pies) were brought over from the Southern states and have remained a very important part of Texas culinary history.

Modern – Representing the United States to date

As Texas culture continues to progress, we are afforded the opportunity to entertain individuals from different cultures. As Texans, we embrace all newcomers and tend to absorb the best regarding food and culture.

As mentioned earlier, Chili Con Carne is the state food of Texas. The state vegetable is the 1015 Onion. The state dessert is pecan pie which makes sense since the state tree is a Pecan tree.

There are many foods that are considered essential Texas foods, but everyone's list might be a little different.

Some iconic Texas Foods and Beverages:

- Barbecue
- Chili
- Chicken Fried Steak
- Queso
- Dr. Pepper
- Blue Bell Ice Cream
- Kolaches
- Sweet Tea
- Fair Food
- King Ranch Casserole
- Breakfast tacos
- Pecan Pie
- Frozen Margaritas
- Whataburger
- fajitas
- buttermilk pie
- catfish

Parker Family Dog Trot Cabin

Chapter Two
A Little Texas Family History

I am a 5th generation Texan and my husband is a 6th generation. According to him, my family would be considered, "Johnny come lately" because the Crowsons arrived in Texas approximately 1837 while his mother's family, the Parkers, arrived in 1834. Both of our families are certified Texas First Families. (To qualify for a Texas First Families Certificate, direct or collateral descendants must have settlement or served the Republic of Texas before February 19, 1846.)

And both families, Parkers and Crowsons, came to America in the 1600's, had at least one ancestor who fought in the Revolutionary War, several in the Civil War, WWI and WWII: among others.

Texas family history is near and dear to both my husband's and my heart. Our families helped initiate some of the infrastructure of this great State and were involved in many stories popular in history books as well as around campfires when those same stories grew dramatically. For the purposes of this book, I will attempt to remain factual but make no promises because most of the stories are best told by older relatives who have a tendency to embellish or fill in the details that may or may not be found in the history books.

Parker Family

My husband, Byron Parker Gentry is the son of Billie Ray Parker Gentry, directly descended from one of Texas's most influential leaders. Daniel Parker (1781-1844) was born to one of the four Parker families listed as Founders and Early Settlers of Texas. Daniel was an early American leader in the Primitive Baptist Church in Elkhart, Texas.

Daniel was born in Culpepper County, Virginia and was the oldest son of John and Sarah Parker. He migrated to Texas in 1834. At the time Daniel wanted to come to Texas, the state was still part of Mexico and the government would not allow any protestant church to be established here. He was determined to establish a church in Texas. On July 26, 1833 in Lamotte, Illinois, he organized and chartered the Pilgrim Predestinarian Regular Baptist Church which he would move to Texas. The church still exists today, near Elkhart, Texas. Daniel was one of the most important frontier preachers in Texas during his time.

Daniel Parker's son, Dickerson Parker was a veteran of the Battle of San Jacinto as well as others. He received a land grant for his service in the Texas army that included the Bachman Lake area in Dallas. His name is carved on the San Jacinto monument along with the other veterans of that battle.

Perhaps the best-known story of the Parker family centered around Cynthia Ann Parker and her brother, John Richard Parker who were kidnapped during a Comanche raid on Fort Parker. Cynthia Ann was ten years old and her brother five years old when the raid occurred. During the Indian raids, many captive children were either adopted or enslaved. Luckily, the Parker children were adopted by the Indians and taught the language and customs of the Indian culture.

As Cynthia Ann grew to young womanhood, she was eventually courted and married to a Comanche chief, Peta Nocona, and bore him 3 children. In all, Cynthia lived with the Indians for about 24 years. An interesting tidbit of Texas history was that Cynthia's son,

Quanah Parker, would later become the last free Comanche Chief who eventually made an agreement to migrate to a reservation in Oklahoma. Quanah and his family continued to prosper and have great influence in both his father's Indian nation and his mother's culture.

When Cynthia Ann was 34 years old, she was discovered by Texas Rangers and ultimately returned to her Parker relatives. She brought along with her, her youngest child, a girl name Topusana (loosely translated as Prairie Flower). Cynthia's uncles, Isaac Duke Parker and Benjamin F Parker were made Cynthia's legal guardians.

Although the return to her family captured the nation's attention and imagination, she never fully recovered from separation from the Indians nor did she ever re-acclimate to society. She grieved for her husband and sons and in 1864, her daughter Topusana caught influenza and died from pneumonia complications. Losing the only child remaining in her care caused Cynthia Ann catastrophic grief. Cynthia died in March of 1871.

In 1910, Quanah Parker moved his mother's and what he thought were his sister's remains to the Post Oak Mission cemetery near Cache, Oklahoma. When Quanah died in February of 1911, he was buried next to them.

Cynthia's brother, John Richard, was ransomed by the Comanche in 1842, but he returned to the Native American society of his own free will some time shortly after his separation from them. Once he returned to the Indians, John participated in raids into Mexico. He contracted Smallpox and was left behind by the Comanches, in a village, with a Mexican slave girl who had also been captured during a raid, and who nursed him back to health. John returned the girl to her family and eventually married her. He returned to the United States during the Civil War and served with Confederate troops. After the war, he returned to Mexico where he died on his ranch in 1915.

Notable Parkers

Isaac Parker (Cynthia Ann's uncle and guardian), was a State Senator. Isaac's home, a beautiful example of a Southern dog trot cabin, is still intact and exhibited at the Log Cabin Village in Fort Worth, Texas.

Elder Ben Parker (son of Daniel Parker) succeeded his father as pastor of the church and was eventually elected to the State Legislature and served there for four years. His early career was as an educator and after studying law and engineering, was a valuable man throughout the eastern part of Texas.

Ira Parker (son of Dickerson Parker) served in the Texas Brigade, was wounded in the Battle of Chickamauga while carrying the Confederate flag, died of his wounds and is buried in Augusta, Georgia.

Bonnie Elizabeth Parker (of the notorious Bonnie & Clyde gang) was a distant relative, not a direct ascendant of our line of Parkers. My sister-in-law says it's not clear how close her relation is. Texas Ranger, Frank Hamer, chased the duo for one hundred and two days and across fifteen states until the duo was ambushed in Louisiana and killed. Allegedly, Bonnie participated in the killing of thirteen people during the gang's murderous spree. I say allegedly, because she didn't survive to go on trial. It's reported that Bonnie had been shot 53 times while Clyde was only hit by 51 bullets.

Crowson Family

The Crowson family is best known for ranching, farming, and later education and law enforcement. Like many during the early years, the Crowsons migrated to Texas, received land grants, and began cultivating crops for sale and personal sustenance. Two of the first Crowsons to arrive were brothers, John Jasper and William Samuel Crowson. The families focused on growing enough fruits and vegetables to feed their families as well as have additional for sale to neighbors and people in town.

After the Civil War, many decided cattle ranching was the business to be in and converted many of their pastures to that pursuit. Somewhat differently than many of their neighbors, the Crowsons were almost a self-sufficient family community, because they continued to farm some of their land. Doing so allowed the Crowsons to prosper through the sale of cattle and vegetables, where others during that time merely existed and often had to pursue other work to supplement their farms and ranches.

The Crowson family had plenty of land and chose to support migrant workers, or share-croppers, who received use of a small plot of land on which they could grow crops for personal use or to sell while they also worked the fields for the Crowson family.

Notable Crowsons

Aaron Crowson (1774-1849) was born in Sevier, Tennessee and married Rhoda Lovelady Crowson in 1819. His grave marker showed he was the "First White Settler in Crowson Cove", Wears Valley, Tennessee in 1792. Aaron and Rhoda lived in Tennessee until his death, after which she moved to Houston County, Texas. The town of Lovelady was name after Rhoda's family. Aaron and Rhoda had eight children, one of whom I am directly descended from. While Rhoda moved to Houston County, following her husband's demise, there were no records found that showed the actual date she arrived.

John Jasper Crowson was born about 1802 in Alabama. He applied for a second-class land grant in on July 5th, 1838 for land in Montgomery County, Texas. Second class grants were issued to citizens living in Texas after March 2, 136 but prior to October 1, 1837. John served under Colonel Jos L Bennet in the Somervell Campaign. He served from October 1, 1842 until January 1, 1843 when he was honorably discharged. John re-enlisted for the Mexican American War and is listed with his brother, William Samuel Crowson, on the Master Rolls of the Texas Units of Veterans in the Mexican American War. He served in Middleton P Johnson's company. The Mexican American War was an armed conflict between the United States and Mexico, from 1846 through 1848. According to the information on the Daughters of the Republic of Texas website, John was killed in battle just a few months before his daughter (Sarah Elizabeth Jane Crowson) was born.

William Samuel Crowson, who joined his brother in service in the Mexican American War, was honorably discharged with disability in 1848. He later served in the Seventeenth Texas Cavalry (Moore's Regiment) from June of 1862 through June of 1863. The Seventeenth Texas Cavalry mustered into Confederate service at Dallas in March of 1862. The regiment defended Fort Hindeman in January of 1863. The five-thousand-man garrison was attacked by a force of thirty thousand. William Samuel appeared on a Roll of Prisoner of War at Camp Douglas and was believed to have survived the fight. Records of burials listed him as dying on January 31, 1863, possibly due to illness or injury complications.

Obediah Lovelady Crowson (March 1832-November 1901) was a Sergeant (Sgt.) in 13th Texas Cavalry – Company B, serving as a Civil War Soldier from 1861-1862. During the war, he suffered the loss of one eye. After the war, he received a soldier's pension until his death in 1901 at which time he was buried in Lovelady (named after his mother's family), Texas in the Rockland Cemetery with military honors for his service in the war.

Major Joseph Crowson (1900-1934) was a prison guard at the Eastham Unit in Weldon, Texas by Raymond Hamilton, Joe Palmer, Henry Methvin. Bonnie and Clyde aided by Hilton Bybee put a pistol in a pre-determined hiding space and waited in a car nearby. As Crowson rode up on a horse, along with another guard, Olin Bozeman, both were shot during the escape. Bozeman was wounded in the hip and ultimately recovered but Crowson, having been shot point blank in the stomach, later died from pneumonia complications. The Bonnie and Clyde gang were responsible for the murder of law enforcement officers in four states; Arkansas, Missouri, Oklahoma, and Texas (between 1932 and 1934).

The Crowson family had many educators, law officers, and writers who helped form the education system and law enforcement for the State of Texas.

So, although my husband points out that his family arrived before mine in Texas and were very much more influential in many ways, at least nobody in my family participated in killing someone from his family (at least as far as I know).

Chapter Three
Let's Get Started

Appetizers, soups and salads are a great way to start any gathering. Whether you are having a neighborhood get together, football party, holiday gathering or just want to spend some quality time with your family and friends on a Sunday afternoon, it is always a good idea to have some tidbits for folks to snack on before sitting down to a meal.

Football parties are a Texas tradition where everyone comes over to watch the game and partake of mass quantities of nummy snacks. Almost always a casual affair with everyone donning his or her favorite team jersey and jeans. Friends bring their favorite munchies and drinks to add to the larder.

Food choices on football days run the gamut but it's hard to go wrong with cheese balls, homemade guacamole and Pico de Gallo or a layered taco dip with chips. Brisket sliders, chicken wings or ribs help to round out a football buffet.

Another great way to meet your neighbors and have friends over is to host a "porch party"; an informal gathering to celebrate some event or holiday by watching a parade from the porch and front yard. Living on Main Street in Waxahachie has prompted many porch parties at our house, including celebrations of Halloween, Veteran's Day, July 4th, and Christmas, to name a few. Families attend with their children and sit on lawn chairs eating delicious food and chatting about the latest news.

The casual atmosphere of a porch party encourages each guest to participate in the event, come and go in the yard, on the porch and throughout the house. At a recent gathering, my husband and I had several people, strangers, who just walked up, introduced themselves and said they had always wanted to see the inside of one of the historical homes on Main Street. We invited them in and showed them around the house while our guests chatted outside. Another lady asked if she could heat her baby's formula in our microwave. She and I introduced ourselves and I showed her through the house, ending up in the kitchen where we chatted while the milk warmed. Three days later, I received the sweetest thank you note from her. People in Texas genuinely care about each other and take the time to be gracious in social situations.

Food at the porch party consists of appetizers, sandwiches, salads, chips and dips and an abundance of desserts. Wintertime events often include chili or soup, served with cornbread and accompaniments to warm the tummies of those attending a colder event like Halloween or Christmas parade. Beverages run the gamut from iced tea (sweet or unsweet), flavored waters, wine, beer or sodas. At Christmas, my husband makes a robust eggnog.

Most of the preparations are handled prior to the party so that we can enjoy spending time with everyone watching the parade. Many times, following the parade or event, everyone will pitch in and help tidy up before heading out to other obligations.

Almost any gathering is made more special with the right appetizers and atmosphere. Good food that flows nicely and hosts that work to make sure each guest feels special and comfortable sets the stage for a successful event.

Appetizers require less time to prepare and allow you to get food in front of your guests immediately. They also give you additional time to finish the preparations for the remainder of the meal. A small serving of food; just a few bites, is meant to reduce hunger and encourage guests to mingle and socialize with each other.

Appetizers require planning, like any part of a menu.

Answering a few key questions enables the host to provide a proper amount and flow of food.

How many types of appetizers should you prepare?
8-10 guests = 3 types
14-16 guests = 4-5 types
Between 16 and up to 45 guests = 6 types
Over 45 guests = 8 types

When do I serve appetizers and how many per person?

Cocktail hour or 30-60 minutes before dinner (plan on 2-4 pieces per person)

1.5-2-hour event preceding dinner (plan on 5-6 pieces per person)

2-4-hour event (light or no dinner), (plan on 8-10 pieces per person)

4+-hour event (with no dinner), (plan on 12-15 pieces per person)

Some of my favorite "go to" appetizers: •Baby Girl's Cheese Ball •Stuffed Mexi-Mushrooms •Layered Crab Dip •Guacamole, Salsa, and Pico de Gallo •Baked Chicken Wings •White or Regular Queso

Shrimp Dip

8 oz. cream cheese, room temperature
½ pound cooked, shelled, and chopped small shrimp (save a couple of the small shrimp whole for garnish)
¼ cup sour cream or Greek yogurt
1 tablespoon lemon juice
1-2 tablespoons toasted slivered almonds
3 tablespoons finely chopped green onions
1 tablespoon milk
¼ to ½ teaspoon crushed red pepper (start with ¼ teaspoon, taste and if you would like additional heat, add another ¼ teaspoon)
Salt to taste

Beat cream cheese and sour cream with a mixer on medium-high until fluffy or about one minute. Stir in lemon juice, onions, pepper, milk and shrimp saving a few whole small shrimp for garnish. Salt and pepper, to taste. Top with roasted almonds. Chill 3-4 hours.

This yummy dip is better with plain crackers. Heap a spoonful on top of a saltine cracker and just pop it into your mouth.

Love Dip

The name of this dip was based on a sleepover my daughter had when she was a teenager. I didn't have much in the house and put together this dip with what I found in the fridge. All evening, one of my daughter's friends kept saying, "mmm...Love Dip!". After about the 3rd time she said it, I decided that I would make this again and it would forever be known as "Love Dip".

16 oz. cream cheese, room temperature (two 8 oz. packages)
¾ teaspoon coarse salt
½ cup green onions, finely chopped (plus more for garnish)
½ cup medium salsa

Beat cream cheese with a mixer on medium-high until fluffy, or about one minute. Beat in salt and green onions. Fold in salsa. Put in a nice serving bowl and top with additional green onions if desired.

Serve with potato chips, corn tortilla chips or assorted crackers.

Baby Girl's Cheese Ball

Baby Girl's Cheese Ball

The most requested recipe, and by far the easiest to prepare was, "Baby Girl's Cheese Ball". Named for my daughter, Raychal, it was a staple at every family gathering.

One of my favorite memories was the time I walked into the kitchen, having just pulled the cheese ball out of the refrigerator ten minutes prior, only to find my teenage daughter sitting on a stool with spoon in hand, eating large chunks of the cheese ball. The look of shock on my face must have been intense because she immediately blushed profusely and defensively said, "What?! You know I don't like crackers!". To this day, I love to make her an extra cheese ball to take home to share with her family so that she remembers how much she is loved, even when she eats a cheese ball with a spoon!

16 oz. cream cheese, room temperature (two 8 oz. packages)
3 to 5 ounces of deli thin meat (smoked ham is a favorite)
3 green onions, chopped tops and bottoms
½ cup chopped pecans

Place cream cheese in a large mixing bowl. Finely chop the deli meat and add to the cream cheese. Add the chopped green onions and mix until well combined. Using clean hands, form into a ball and roll in chopped pecans.

Refrigerate until 20 minutes before you are ready to serve it with assorted crackers on a decorative plate or platter.

The easiest recipes are often the ones that guests request the most. Every time I've taken this to a function, at least two or three people ask for the recipe.

Note: During the holidays, it is fun to make cheese balls with the nuts mixed in with the cheese then roll one cheese ball in chopped parsley and another in paprika. Looks festive and gives them a slightly different taste.

Four Layer Crab Dip

Four Layer Crab Dip

Layer One
8 oz. cream cheese, room temperature
¼ cup mayonnaise
Juice from half of a medium-size lemon

In a small mixing bowl, blend the cream cheese, mayonnaise, and lemon juice until well combined. Spread in a round 10" quiche dish with fluted edges or a clear glass pie pan.

Layer Two
Cocktail Sauce
1 cup ketchup
1 tablespoon horseradish
1 tablespoon lemon juice
1 tablespoon Worcestershire sauce
¼ teaspoon salt
1/8 teaspoon black pepper
1 to 4 dashes hot sauce (I use Tabasco or Louisiana, use *your* favorite)

In a separate bowl, combine all ingredients, taste and add additional hot sauce to taste. Spread about half of the cocktail sauce over the cream cheese layer.

Layer Three
1-pound fresh lump crab meat

Sprinkle crab meat over the sauce layer until sauce is fully covered.

Layer Four
1 bunch fresh curly parsley

Place parsley over the crab meat until all crab is covered.

Serve the layered dip with assorted crackers. Butter crackers make a nice compliment to this appetizer.

Cheese Crisp Cookies

Cheese straws are served at gatherings all around the South. This recipe is similar but results in a single heavenly bite of crispy cheese cookie instead of a formed cheese straw. Enjoy these with cocktails or just for snacks.

2 sticks (1 cup) unsalted butter, softened
2 cups all-purpose flour
2 cups grated cheddar cheese (mild or sharp)
4 cups puffed rice cereal
½ teaspoon ground red pepper

Preheat oven to 325 degrees. Line a baking sheet with parchment paper. Combine all ingredients and form into little balls about 1" in diameter and place on sheet about 1" apart.

Flatten with a fork that has been dipped in water. Bake at 325 degrees for 12-14 minutes or until lightly browned. Cool cookies on a baking rack and store in an airtight container

Creamy Dreamy Queso

1 lb. processed cheese spread (16 oz. Velveeta)
14 oz. can of mild tomatoes with green chilis (I use Rotel "Hot")
3 teaspoons sour cream
4 oz. cream cheese
¼ cup cheddar cheese, shredded
**jalapeno, minced (optional if you'd like additional heat)

Cut Velveeta into cubes for easier melting. In a saucepan, over low to medium heat, put ingredients in pan, stir continuously until all ingredients are melted and fully combined.

Taste, and if additional heat is desired, add 1/2 a teaspoon of minced jalapeno at a time until the desired heat level is achieved.

Serve with tortilla chips, quesadillas, tacos, or almost anything you eat!

White Queso

1 lb. Velveeta Queso Blanco cheese
½ cup milk or half and half
1 tablespoon butter
½ of a 4 oz. can of green chilies (I use Rotel "hot")
1 tablespoon pickled jalapenos
¼ teaspoon taco seasoning
1/8 teaspoon garlic powder

Cut Velveeta in small cubes for easier melting. In a saucepan, over low to medium heat, put all ingredients in pan, stir continuously until all ingredients are melted and fully combined.

Taste, and if additional heat is desired, add 1/2 a teaspoon of minced jalapeno at a time until the desired heat level is achieved.

Serve with tortilla chips, quesadillas, tacos, or almost anything you eat!

Guacamole

2 avocados, peeled, de-seeded, and mashed
1 medium tomato, chopped small
½ cup onion, chopped small
1 teaspoon lime juice or up to ½ lime's juice
1 jalapeno pepper, chopped small (OR ½ small serrano chopped small)
¼ teaspoon garlic powder
Salt & Pepper, to taste

    Peel and mash avocados. Combine all ingredients then salt and pepper to taste. Serve with any Mexican food or as an appetizer with tortilla chips.

Lazy Day Guacamole

    Having a lazy day and want some guacamole?! Simply mash two avocados, add **3 or 4 tablespoons of Pico de Gallo**; stir to combine and **salt/pepper to taste**. This is what we call shortcut guacamole at our house.

Pico de Gallo

This is actually my husband's recipe. Our family and friends always enjoy his Pico and Guacamole when we get together for an enchilada feast.

The only negative about Byron's Pico and Guacamole is that by the time I finished making the enchiladas, everyone was starting to feel full because nobody could stop eating his treats until the bowls were empty.

1 large tomato, chopped small
½ medium onion, chopped small
1 small serrano pepper, minced
½ bunch of fresh cilantro (chopped)
Juice of half of a lime
Salt to taste

Chop tomato and onion and put in a small mixing bowl. Add serrano pepper, cilantro and lime juice. Sprinkle with salt, taste and add additional salt if necessary.

Serve with tortilla chips or as a condiment. Great in scrambled eggs for breakfast or as an accompaniment to any Mexican food meal.

Tomatillo Salsa

15 fresh tomatillos, husks removed
1 cup Vidalia onion, chopped
1 cup fresh cilantro, chopped
1 teaspoon salt
1/2 teaspoon ground black pepper

Place tomatillos in a saucepan and add enough water to cover. Bring to a boil, cook for 7 minutes. Turn off heat and let stand for about 10 minutes; drain and cool.

Combine cooled tomatillos and remaining ingredients in a blender or food processor and pulse 6 to 8 times or until desired consistency. Cover and chill. Serve with tortilla chips.

Quick Salsa

14.5 oz. can diced tomatoes
14.5 oz. can diced tomatoes with green peppers and onion
4 oz. can chopped green chilis
1 Vidalia onion, chopped
2 jalapeno peppers, seeded and chopped
1 lime, juiced
1 ½ teaspoons salt
¾ teaspoon ground black pepper

Combine all ingredients in a blender or food processor, and pulse 6 to 8 times, or until desired consistency. Cover and chill. Serve with tortilla chips.

Mexi-Mushrooms

My daughter doesn't like bacon so I often fry breakfast sausage for her. When I make Mexi-Mushrooms for Raychal I substitute ½ cup of this sausage broken up in place of the bacon listed below. The remainder of the recipe is unchanged. This recipe is easily doubled to serve as an appetizer at a cocktail party. Make plenty as these mushrooms will disappear quickly and guests are always eager for more.

21 White or Cremini Mushrooms (cleaned, with stems removed)
8 oz. cream cheese, room temperature
8 bacon slices (cooked and crumbled)
1 cup cheddar cheese, shredded
4 oz. can minced jalapenos (drained and rinsed)
2 cloves garlic, minced
Salt & Pepper to taste
Optional: additional cheddar cheese for topping if desired
Optional: green onions, finely chopped (for garnish)

Preheat oven to 400 degrees. Line a rimmed baking sheet with parchment paper or foil and set aside.

To a small mixing bowl, combine cream cheese bacon, shredded cheddar cheese, jalapenos, garlic, salt and pepper. Stir well.

Spoon approximately 1 tablespoon of the filling mixture into each mushroom cap. Top with additional cheese, if desired. Bake 20-25 minutes or until mushrooms are piping hot and cheese is melted and turning a light golden color.

Carefully remove the mushrooms from the baking sheet with a spatula and let sit at room temperature on serving plate for about 5 minutes. Serve sprinkled with green onions.

Baked Chicken Wings

2 pounds chicken wings
2 tablespoons unsalted butter, melted
1 tablespoon vegetable oil
1 teaspoon garlic powder
Salt & Pepper to taste
1 tablespoon fresh cilantro, chopped (garnish after broiling)

Preheat oven to 400 degrees and line a baking sheet with parchment paper then set aside.

In a large mixing bowl, combine the melted butter, vegetable oil, garlic powder, salt and pepper. Stir to fully combine. Add chicken and toss until fully coated on all sides.

Place chicken pieces on parchment covered baking sheet and bake at 400 degrees for 25-30 minutes, turning chicken midway.

Glaze:

5 tablespoons unsalted butter, melted
1 tablespoon all-purpose flour
¼ cup honey
¼ cup sriracha sauce
1 tablespoon soy sauce
Juice of 1 lime

Melt butter in small saucepan over medium heat. Whisk in flour, about 1 minute. Stir in honey, Sriracha, soy sauce and lime juice. Bring to a boil, simmer until thickened.

Once chicken wings are cooked, brush with glaze and return to broil for 3-4 minutes or until crisp and crusted. Garnish with cilantro.

Brie en Croute

1 sheet frozen puff pastry
1 tablespoon unsalted butter
½ cup walnuts or pecans
1/8 teaspoon ground cinnamon
8 oz. wheel of Brie or Camembert
¼ cup brown sugar
1 egg, beaten

Preheat oven to 375 degrees. Defrost puff pastry for 15 to 20 minutes and unfold.

In a saucepan, melt butter over medium heat. Sauté pecans/walnuts in the butter until golden brown, approximately 3 – 5 minutes. Add the cinnamon and stir until nuts are coated well. Place the nut mixture on top of the Brie and sprinkle brown sugar over the mixture.

Lay the puff pastry on a flat surface and place Brie/Camembert in the center. Gather up the edges of the pastry and press around the cheese. Gently squeeze together excess dough and tie together with a piece of kitchen twine OR simply twist the top so it will not open when baked.

Brush the beaten egg over top and sides. Place the cheese on a cookie sheet and bake or 20 minutes, until the pastry is golden.

Baked Brie or Camembert

8 oz. Brie or Camembert cheese round
1 tablespoon unsalted butter, softened
¼ cup sliced almonds

Preheat oven to 350 degrees. Remove cheese from box/wrapping and rub butter over the outside of the cheese rind. Place buttered cheese round into a 5" cast iron skillet and sprinkle with almond slices.

Bake cheese for 12-15 minutes, only until the cheese has started to melt. Serve with slices of French baguette, apples and pears.

Jam & Brie Tarts

These little gems are so tasty, serve them with champagne or hot cider, depending on the occasion.

1 package (1.9 ounces) frozen miniature phyllo tart shells
3 tablespoons crushed gingersnaps
6 oz. Brie or Camembert cheese, rind removed and cubed
¼ cup spreadable fruit of your choice (*Apricot preserves or orange marmalade compliment the gingersnaps*)

Place the tart shells on an ungreased baking sheet. Sprinkle about ½ teaspoon gingersnap crumbs into each shell. Top with brie cube and spreadable fruit. Bake at 325 degrees for 5 minutes or until cheese is melted.

Cheese and Honey Fondue

1 cup heavy cream
1 cup chicken broth
1 tablespoon honey
2 cups freshly shredded Jarlsberg cheese
½ cup freshly shredded Swiss cheese
¼ cup all-purpose flour
¼ teaspoon dry mustard
¼ teaspoon cracked black pepper

In a medium saucepan, bring heavy cream, chicken broth, and honey to a boil over medium to medium-low heat.

In a mixing bowl, combine cheeses, flour, mustard and pepper. Slowly whisk cheese mixture into simmering broth until melted and smooth. Transfer to a fondue pot; keep warm.

Serve with cubed ciabatta bread, French bread, sliced pears or apples, celery and/or crackers.

Strawberry Soup

2 cups hulled and sliced strawberries
1 cup orange juice
1 cup vanilla yogurt
½ teaspoon vanilla extract
Mint leaves (optional)

In a blender or food processor, combine all ingredients except mint and process until smooth.

Ladle the soup into bowls and garnish with mint (if desired) or a dollop of yogurt. This soup is best served chilled for at least an hour before serving. It's especially refreshing during the summer months.

Pumpkin Soup

1 medium onion, chopped
1 lb. mushrooms, chopped
½ cup butter (1 stick)
1/3 cup flour
2 quarts low sodium chicken broth or stock
2 cups pumpkin
2 cups heavy cream
2 teaspoons honey
1 teaspoon curry
Salt and Pepper to taste

In a large pot, sauté onions and mushrooms in butter. Add flour and cook, stirring until smooth. Add chicken broth or stock, pumpkin, cream, honey, curry, salt and pepper. Simmer for 30-45 minutes to blend all ingredients. Great served with homemade bread.

Corn and Crab Bisque

2 cups fresh corn, cut from cob (about 6 ears)
3 ¾ cups no salt added chicken broth
1 tablespoon vegetable oil
1 cup chopped onion
3 cloves garlic, minced
3 ¾ cups milk (or a mixture of milk and half and half), divided
½ teaspoon ground pepper
¼ teaspoon salt
½ teaspoon hot sauce
½ cup all-purpose flour
1 lb. fresh lump crab meat
Paprika, for garnish

Combine corn and chicken broth in a large saucepan or Dutch oven. Bring to a boil over medium high heat, stirring occasionally. Reduce heat and simmer for 20 minutes.

Coat a small skillet with cooking spray, add oil and place over medium high heat until hot. Add onion, and follow that, the garlic. Add onion mixture to corn and chicken broth, 3 ¼ cups milk, the next 3 ingredients. In a small saucepan or skillet, combine with remaining ½ cup milk and flour, cooking until thickened. Add this to the corn and chicken broth then add crab meat. Simmer until ready to serve. Yummy with cheddar biscuits.

Hearty Beef Stew

6 oz. bacon, chopped into small pieces
2 tablespoons olive oil
2 lbs. beef stew meat (beef chuck 1" pieces)
2 ½ teaspoons salt
1 ½ teaspoons black pepper
¼ cup all-purpose flour
1 cup dry red wine
1 lb. mushrooms, thickly sliced
4 carrots, peeled and cut into ½" slices
1 medium onion, diced
4 garlic cloves, minced
1 tablespoon tomato paste
4 cups low sodium beef broth or stock
2 bay leaves
½ teaspoon dried thyme
1 lb. small potatoes (use new potatoes, fingerling halved or quartered)

In a large Dutch oven, sauté bacon over medium heat until browned. Use a slotted spoon to remove bacon and set aside.

While bacon is cooking, put beef in a large mixing bowl and season with 1 ½ teaspoons of salt and 1 teaspoon of black pepper.

Sprinkle beef with ¼ cup flour and toss to coat.

Transfer beef to hot bacon fat (will probably need to be done in two batches) and cook over medium-high heat until the beef is browned on all sides (about 3 minutes per side). Add additional oil if needed.

Place the cooked beef in the same bowl as bacon.

Add 2 cups of wine to the pot and bring to a boil, scraping all the beef bits from the bottom of the pot. Add sliced mushrooms and simmer over medium heat for about 10 minutes.

Heat a large non-stick skillet over medium-high heat and add 2 tablespoons olive oil. Add sliced carrots, diced onion, and chopped garlic, sautéing for 3-4 minutes. Add tomato paste and sauté another minute or two.

Transfer vegetables to the soup pot.

Add beef broth, bay leaves, thyme, 1 teaspoon salt and ½ teaspoon pepper. Return beef and bacon to the pot then add potatoes.

Stir to combine and make sure all potatoes are covered.

Bake at 325 degrees for 1 hour and 30 minutes.

30-Minute Tortilla Soup

This has always been a winter staple at our house. It's easy to make and fast. I'd make it at midday, then put it on low simmer when its finished. As each family member got home, they would serve themselves a hearty bowl. Ready in thirty minutes but tastes like you've been cooking all day.

Soup
2 tablespoons olive oil
1 cup chopped onion
2 cloves garlic, minced
1 large jalapeno, diced
32 oz. low sodium chicken broth
two 14.5 oz. cans diced tomatoes and juice
1 can black beans, drained
2 cups shredded chicken
1 ½ cups corn (fresh or frozen)
1 tablespoon lime juice
1 tablespoon chili powder
2 teaspoons cumin
1 teaspoon salt (or to taste)
1/2 teaspoon black pepper
1 teaspoon smoked paprika
¼ teaspoon cayenne
1/3 cup fresh cilantro leaves, chopped
Diced avocado (garnish)
Shredded cheddar cheese (garnish).

Fry the tortilla strips first and set aside (see next page).

In a large Dutch oven or deep saucepan, add olive oil and heat over medium. Add chopped onion and jalapeno, cooking until the onion starts to become tender. Add garlic, chicken broth, tomatoes, beans, corn, lime juice, and seasonings to the pot. Reduce the heat to low and last, add chicken and tortilla strips, reserving a few strips to garnish each bowl. Simmer at least 20 minutes or until ready to serve.

Garnish the soup with diced avocado, cheese and/or tomatoes and serve with additional tortillas for dipping into the soup.

Tortilla Strips

10 small tortillas, cut into strips
2 tablespoons olive oil
1 teaspoon Kosher salt

Fry tortilla strips in olive oil, Remove with slotted spoon onto paper towels and sprinkle with salt. Set aside.

Creole Gumbo

¾ stick of unsalted butter
2 cups chopped green onions, tops and bottoms
2 cups sliced okra, fresh or frozen
1 cup chopped white onions
2 cups raw, peeled shrimp, small to small-medium in size
2 cups raw oysters
1 cup crushed tomato with juice
1 cup tomato juice (Clamato works well)
1 ½ quarts fish stock
3 crabs (top shell should be discarded, cut into 4 pieces
3 tablespoons flour
1 tablespoon gumbo file'
3 cups cooked rice
Salt and pepper, to taste
Cayenne pepper, to taste

In a large Dutch oven, melt the butter and sauté the green onions, okra, white onions and crabs. In a separate pot, put the shrimp, oysters, tomatoes, and tomato juice in with the fish stock and bring to a boil. Let boil for a minute, then add to the Dutch oven.

In a small skillet, cook the butter and flour together to make a roux. Stir and cook until roux is light brown in color. Blend this brown roux with the file and some of the gumbo liquid then add back to pot. Add salt, pepper and cayenne, to taste. Simmer on low heat for 1 ½ hours.

Serve with cooked (boiled or steamed) rice and French bread.

Bebe's Favorite Chicken Salad

3 boneless chicken breasts (boiled and chopped)
½ cup finely diced celery
¼ cup green onions, tops and bottoms
½ cup seedless red grapes, each cut in half
6 tablespoons (3/8 cup) mayonnaise
6 tablespoons (3/8 cup) Greek yogurt
Salt and Pepper to taste
½ cup almonds or pecans (optional)

Stir together all ingredients and chill for at least an hour before serving.

I boil my chicken breasts in chicken stock for a richer chicken flavor. This chicken salad is fantastic for crustless tea sandwiches or on top of mixed greens.

Ham and Blue Cheese Pasta Salad

3 cups dried bowtie or wheel pasta (measure prior to cooking)
1 cup coarsely chopped pecans, toasted
1/3 cup parmesan cheese, grated
2 tablespoons chopped fresh parsley
1 tablespoon minced fresh rosemary
½ to ¾ teaspoon black pepper
4 ounces cooked ham, cut into bite-sized strips
4 ounces blue cheese crumbles
1 garlic clove, minced
¼ cup olive oil

Cook pasta according to package directions. Drain well and place pasta in large serving bowl. Add pecans and next seven ingredients, tossing gently to combine. Add oil, stir to coat mixture.

Serve immediately or cover and chill until ready to serve.

Blue Cheese Dressing

½ cup mayonnaise
½ cup Greek yogurt or sour cream
1 teaspoon celery salt
2 teaspoons freshly squeezed lime juice
2 teaspoons Dijon mustard
1 tablespoon minced onion
1 tablespoon minced fresh tarragon
1 teaspoon Tabasco or other hot sauce
3 to 4 ounces blue cheese crumbles

Mix all ingredients, except blue cheese crumbles and process in food processor until smooth. Add blue cheese crumbles and pulse a few times, leaving cheese lumpy.

This dressing is rich and creamy and has a lovely texture. Serve over wedge salad with steak or over spinach salad with boiled eggs.

Cranberry Marshmallow Salad

12 oz. fresh cranberries
½ cup sugar
8 oz. crushed pineapple, drained
2 cups mini marshmallows
1 cup heavy cream
½ cup chopped pecans

Pulse cranberries in a food processor until chopped. Add chopped cranberries to a medium mixing bowl and mix in sugar. Refrigerate overnight. Whip heavy cream to stiff peaks, add nuts and refrigerate until ready to serve.

Spinach Salad with Hot Bacon Dressing

1 package baby spinach
1 small purple onion, sliced thin
3 eggs, boiled, peeled and sliced
½ small carton mushrooms, sliced

Layer salad ingredients in above order and chill while making dressing.

Hot Bacon Dressing:

4 slices bacon
2 tablespoons sugar
2 tablespoons all-purpose flour
1 egg, beaten
2 tablespoons cider vinegar
¼ cup water
¾ cup milk

Cook bacon until crisp and remove from pan. Set aside to cool. In a small bowl, mix sugar, flour, egg and vinegar. Poor ingredients into the cooled bacon skillet and cook over low heat until thickened. Crumble half of the cooked bacon and put on the salad greens. Crumble the remaining half of bacon and return to the dressing skillet. Simmer the hot bacon dressing until thickened. Salt and pepper to taste.

The dressing will slightly wilt the salad and it should be served and eaten while the dressing is warm. In serving this, I usually pour 1/3 of the dressing over salad and serve the remainder in a gravy boat.

The dressing can be refrigerated for up to one week.

Spinach Apricot Salad

1 cup boiling water
6 oz. package dried apricots, cut in half
1 lb. baby spinach
3 tablespoons cider vinegar
3 tablespoons apricot preserves
½ cup vegetable oil
¾ cup coarsely chopped macadamia nuts, toasted

In a small bowl, pour boiling water over cut apricots and let soak for 30 minutes; drain well. Wash and dry spinach. Combine vinegar and preserves in blender and process until smooth. With blender on high, gradually add oil.

Combine spinach, half of apricots, half of nuts and dressing. Toss and sprinkle with remaining nuts and apricots.

Broccoli Salad

2 heads of broccoli, cut into florets and discard stems
1 cup raisins
1 cup sunflower seeds
½ cup chopped onion
½ apple, chopped
1 cup Miracle Whip or Mayonnaise
½ cup sugar
1 tablespoon vinegar

Mix broccoli, raisins, sunflower seeds, and onion together. In a separate bowl, mix mayonnaise, sugar, and vinegar together and pour over salad. Toss to combine and chill until ready to serve.

This salad is especially nice in the summer as a side dish for barbecue or hamburgers.

Cole Slaw

1 large bag Cole slaw mixture (white/purple cabbage, carrots)
1/8 teaspoon garlic powder
½ cup mayonnaise (or more as desired)
¼ cup vinegar
¼ cup sugar
1 teaspoon lemon juice
Salt and pepper, to taste

Mix garlic powder, mayonnaise, vinegar, sugar, lemon juice and salt and pepper. Pour dressing over Cole slaw mixture and toss to combine. Best if refrigerated for a minimum 2 hours prior to serving.

I like to add half of a green bell pepper, diced, to the salad mixture. I also sprinkle a touch of celery salt. Test the consistency and moistness of the Cole slaw and add additional mayonnaise as necessary to achieve the desired consistency.

Cucumbers with Sour Cream Dressing

2 medium cucumbers, peeled, and sliced into rounds
1 sweet onion, sliced into thin rings
2 tablespoons sugar
¼ teaspoon salt
1/8 teaspoon black pepper
½ cup mayonnaise
2 tablespoons white vinegar
3 tablespoons whole milk or half and half

Place cucumbers in a large bowl. Add the onion and toss. Add 1 tablespoon of sugar, salt, and black pepper. Toss to combine. In a separate bowl, combine mayonnaise, remaining sugar, vinegar and milk. Toss together and chill at least 1 hour to marry the ingredients.

Tomato, Avocado and Cucumber Salad

1 lb. Roma tomatoes, chopped into bite-sized pieces
1 English cucumber
½ medium red or purple onion, sliced thinly
2 avocados, diced
2 tablespoons olive oil
Juice of 1 lemon (approximately 2 tablespoons)
¼ cup chopped cilantro
1 teaspoon sea salt
1/8 teaspoon black pepper

    Place chopped tomatoes, sliced cucumber, sliced onion, diced avocados and chopped cilantro into a large salad bowl. Drizzle with 2 tablespoons olive oil and 2 tablespoons lemon juice. Toss to combine. Just before serving, add salt and pepper and toss once again.

Fruited Chicken Salad

4 cups cooked chicken, cubed
2 cups diced celery
2 tablespoon lemon juice
½ cup plain Greek yogurt
½ cup mayonnaise
2 cups halved green or seedless purple grapes
1 cup slivered almonds
Salt and Pepper to taste

    Toss chicken, celery, lemon juice, salt and pepper in a large bowl. Mix in yogurt and mayonnaise, fold in grapes. Cover and chill for at least an hour. Right before serving, sprinkle with almonds.

    This salad is so refreshing for a summer meal. I serve in bib lettuce cups with assorted crackers.

Potato Salad

10 cups cubed red potatoes
3 celery stalks, diced
1 cup diced dill pickles
½ cup diced red onion (or sweet onion like Vidalia)
3 hard-boiled eggs, peeled and diced
1 cup mayonnaise
¼ cup mustard
Salt and Pepper to taste

Cover potatoes with water and bring to a boil. Reduce heat and continue to simmer until potatoes are tender. A fork or knife should be able to slice through the potato without any resistance.

Drain and rinse the potatoes. Cover with cold water until potatoes are cool. Drain again. Mash potatoes and stir together with celery, pickles, onions, eggs, mayonnaise and mustard until combined. Season to taste with salt and pepper. Refrigerate at least an hour or until ready to serve.

Pistachio Fluff

20 oz. can crushed pineapple, well drained
4 oz. pistachio pudding mix
8 oz. whipped cream**
½ cup chopped pecans
1 cup miniature marshmallows

Combine pudding mix, pineapple, nuts, marshmallows and whipped cream. Refrigerate at least 2 hours prior to serving.

**Note: For this recipe, I like to take a cup of heavy cream, add ½ teaspoon vanilla and 1 tablespoon sugar and whip until stiff peaks form. This tastes so much better than using frozen whipped topping.

Tuna Salad

20 ounces tuna, packed in water (four 5 oz. cans), well drained
1 medium onion, diced
1 medium apple, seeded and diced
1 avocado, diced
1 cup mayonnaise
½ teaspoon fresh lemon juice
½ cup sliced almonds or chopped walnuts, toasted
1/8 teaspoon black pepper
Additional salt and pepper to taste

Toast nuts on a dry skillet until fragrant and golden. Remove from heat and set aside to cool.

Drain tuna. Combine all ingredients in a large mixing bowl and add black pepper and lemon juice to taste. Serve in half of an avocado or as a sandwich spread on a croissant with lettuce and tomato.

Orange Vinaigrette

¼ cup white wine or champagne vinegar
2 teaspoons grated orange zest
3 tablespoons fresh orange juice
1 tablespoon sugar
½ teaspoon salt
½ teaspoon black pepper
¾ cup olive oil

Whisk all ingredients until well blended or put all ingredients in a Mason jar and shake until well combined.

This salad dressing is great served over a spinach salad or grilled chicken salad.

Spicy Lime Vinaigrette

3 tablespoons fresh lime juice
2 tablespoons honey
3 tablespoons rice wine vinegar
1 teaspoon Dijon mustard
1/3 cup olive oil
½ teaspoon salt
Optional: 1 teaspoon chipotle in adobo sauce

    Add all ingredients to a blender and pulse until blended or put all ingredients in a Mason jar and shake until thickened and well combined.

I love this dressing over a grilled steak salad.

Layered Oatmeal

Chapter Four

Bread and Breakfast

Childhood memories are so special. One of mine centers around the smell of baking bread early in the morning. Specifically, the nutty smell of flour baking in a hot oven takes me to a simpler time when I sat at my grandmother's (Mamaw's) table and talked to her while she made breakfast for the hardworking cowboys who worked her ranch. Depending on the time of year, those cowboys consisted of uncles, cousins, and my grandfather or in high volume times, they might include neighbors and paid workers.

Deep in the piney woods of East Texas lies the sleepy little town of Lovelady and the bigger town of Crockett. The town of Lovelady was named after Cyrus Lovelady, one of its earlier settlers. The town was founded in 1872 and had a whopping 649 people at the end of the 2010 census. Between Lovelady and Crockett, out in Houston County was a cattle ranch owned by my family.

On a working ranch, a day typically started at 4:30 a.m. for my grandfather or Papaw to those grandchildren who adored him. He would walk out onto the porch each morning, after taking a long drink of buttermilk he'd grabbed from the refrigerator and waited for his help to arrive. Sometimes he used a glass for his buttermilk and sometimes not, and if not my grandmother (Mamaw) would fuss and fan her apron at him to no avail.

Summers were best on the ranch. Crops were growing, calves were walking the pastures and I was in residence until about a week before school started. Mamaw would wake me at about 6:00 a.m. to help her with breakfast. By that time, the activity on the ranch had been going on for quite some time. Papaw always said, "work first, feed those animals, and then we'll eat." He believed in taking care of all the critters on the ranch before the humans. He was tough but fair and his ranch was run with care and firm hand. Mamaw "slept in" until 6:00 a.m. when she got up to make an expansive breakfast for everyone. It amazed me that many days she managed this feat without my or anyone's assistance. It was not unusual to see 8-10 people sitting around the breakfast table on any given morning.

Mamaw made her biscuits in cast iron skillets (yes, it took at least two or three skillets to hold a mornings worth of biscuits). Those lovely treats were crusty and golden on the outside with pillows of soft goodness on the inside. Whoever said breakfast was the most important meal of the day must have known my grandmother. Breakfast usually consisted of two meats, potatoes, eggs, and the best homemade biscuits you've ever eaten. She always had freshly made preserves and sugar syrup on the table. Cracking open a hot biscuit, watching that steam rise, and spreading a thick layer of butter on each side as it is opened across the plate, was a heavenly experience. Pouring hot sugar syrup on top of the biscuits melted the butter and mouths began to water, knowing that there was nothing like that first bite of biscuit soaked in butter and syrup. The smells in Mamaw's kitchen made memories I still carry in my heart. Breakfast at the ranch was one of those experiences that I only close my eyes to relive again and again.

Mamaw would get the bacon and sausage cooking slowly on the back burners of her stovetop and turned on the oven to heat while she started to prepare the biscuit dough. Watching her as she worked the dough made the task appear effortless. Her hands seemed to fly as she worked the fat into the flour mixture until it looked like uniform pea-sized bits of gold. Then she quickly poured buttermilk over the flour and butter mixture and used a fork to mix until all bits were moistened. She turned the dough a few times to build layers as well as incorporate any flour bits. The counter had been prepared with additional flour, so the biscuits never got stuck on the surface. They wouldn't dare in Mamaw's kitchen! She never rolled her dough, she patted the dough into a circle and used a juice glass to make small biscuits. Each biscuit was carefully placed upside down in the cast iron skillet to leave only a little room for hot air to help the biscuits rise. She brushed buttermilk or made an egg wash to clean off excess flour. She baked her biscuits in a hot oven for about thirteen to fifteen minutes or until the tops were golden. Those skillets were so hot and steamy coming out of her oven.

She worked to balance her kitchen to make sure that the biscuits were ready and being passed around the table while she finished the bacon, sausage and eggs. Eggs were always the last item to prepare and were started once all the cowboys were washed up and seated around the table. My grandmother would sit down, reach to the cowboy on each side of her, take hold of their hands and say a quick grace before everyone started eating. My grandfather wasn't a highly religious man but saying the blessing at Mamaw's table was a daily standard. That and listening to the church services each Sunday morning were my grandfather's rituals.

Those cowboys were tough and could handle any challenges on a working ranch, but each took special care with my grandmother and showed the utmost respect at her table.

After gorging themselves, some of the young men would pocket an additional biscuit to help get them through the morning chores. Funny, there were seldom leftovers from breakfast, lunch or dinner at the ranch. Every morning at least one of the cowboys, cousins or neighbors would offer to help clear the table or do dishes but Mamaw never allowed anyone to handle things in her kitchen. She would shoo everyone out and then start cleaning up. Once everyone returned to chores, my grandmother would clean the dishes from the table and head to the sink. While she hummed and washed every dish by hand, she would decide what would be served for lunch. She would barely get through washing the morning dishes before all the preparation work for the next meal would start. I felt lucky in those instances when she would allow me to stand beside her and dry those dishes as she finished washing them.

Mamaw smiled through her days, working hard to provide exceptional meals to support those who handled the cows, horses, and crops. In her mind, gathering family and friends at her table was one of many ways of showing love and affection. Those were good times for grandparents and a summertime country girl.

Mamaw's Biscuits

Biscuits, like Dallas hair, should be a mile high

2 cups all-purpose flour (White Lilly if you can find it)
1 tablespoon baking powder
½ teaspoon salt
5 tablespoons butter (Mamaw used half butter/half lard), frozen
¾ cup buttermilk (add more as necessary, I typically use almost a cup of buttermilk). The dough should stand without sagging but not appear too dry.

Preheat oven to 425 degrees. Biscuits will cook best on the center rack in the oven. Grease a 10" cast iron skillet (or spray with non-stick cooking spray) and set aside while preparing the biscuit dough.

In a large mixing bowl, mix all dry ingredients (flour, baking powder, salt) with a whisk. Grate frozen butter over flour mixture and use a fork to incorporate the butter (avoid touching the butter as it will start to melt if handled). Once the butter is fully mixed with the flour, make a well in the center and pour in the buttermilk.

Keeping all the ingredients cold helps biscuits rise and become fluffy. Again, mix with a fork to avoid handling the dough directly. The more solid and cold the butter, the higher the biscuit.

Sprinkle a little flour on the counter and put dough in the middle of the floured area. Pat the dough gently into a circle about ½" to ¾" thick. Use a 2" biscuit cutter, pushing straight down without twisting. Place the biscuits bottom side up in the skillet, barely touching. The hot air between them helps the rising process.

Brush with either leftover buttermilk or an egg wash (1 egg, beaten with 1 teaspoon water) on top of each biscuit to remove excess flour on the tops. Put the biscuits into the hot oven and bake for approximately 13-15 minutes or until starting to lightly brown on top.

When the biscuits are removed from the oven, brush with melted butter. Move biscuits to a serving platter or lined basket. Serve with additional butter and either jam or sugar syrup.

Sugar Syrup for Biscuits

1 cup sugar
1/2 cup water

To make basic sugar syrup (or simple syrup), put sugar and water in a small saucepan and heat over medium heat until boiling. Boil for about 5 minutes and then reduce heat to simmer while your other food is cooking.

Pour into a syrup pitcher or server and let cool at least 15 minutes before serving. The cooler the syrup gets, the thicker it will become.

Enjoy the syrup "as is" or use one of these additions for a special treat for biscuits, pancakes or French toast.

***Cherry Syrup** – add **½ cup pitted cherries**, cut in half and boil for 5 minutes to soften the fruit. When you remove the syrup from the heat, add **1/4 teaspoon almond extract** to enhance the flavor.

***Strawberry Syrup** – add **½ cup strawberries**, quartered, and boil for 5 minutes to soften the fruit. When you remove the syrup from the heat, add **½ teaspoon vanilla** extract to enhance the flavor.

***Blueberry Syrup** – add **½ cup blueberries**, whole, and boil for 5 minutes to soften the fruit. When you remove the syrup from heat, add **½ teaspoon lemon zest and a squirt of lemon.**

***Blackberry Syrup** – add **½ cup blackberries**, halved, and boil for 5 minutes to soften the fruit. When you remove, add **½ teaspoon lemon zest and a squirt of lemon** juice. You can use orange zest and juice as a substitute if you want it to be a little sweeter.

***Raspberry Syrup** – add **½ cup raspberries**, whole, and boil for 5 minutes to soften the fruit. When you remove, add **½ teaspoon orange zest and a squirt of orange juice**.

***Peach Syrup** – add **1 peach**, pitted and sliced, and boil for 5 minutes to soften the fruit. When you remove, add **½ teaspoon vanilla extract and one "shake" of cinnamon**.

***Banana Syrup** – add **½ of a banana**, sliced, and boil for 5 minutes to soften the fruit. No need to add anything as the banana flavor is intense and tastes great served over French toast or baked pancake.

***Maple Butter Syrup** – after boiling the syrup, add **½ teaspoon maple extract** and one tablespoon of unsalted butter. Stir until fully combined and pour over biscuits or pancakes.

Bebe's Quick Biscuits

2 cups self-rising flour
6 tablespoons butter, frozen
1 tablespoon baking powder
1 teaspoon sugar
1 cup buttermilk (or whole milk if you prefer)

Preheat oven to 425 degrees. In a large mixing bowl, put flour, baking powder, and sugar together and whisk until combined.

Grate frozen butter over flour mixture and incorporate with fork. Pour milk over flour and butter mixture and mix only until combined. Sprinkle flour on the counter and place the dough in the center of the floured area. Pat dough to make a circle approximately ½" to ¾" thick. Using a 2" biscuit cutter, cut biscuits straight down, don't twist the biscuit cutter. Place in a greased 10" cast iron skillet and place in oven for 13-15 minutes or until lightly browned.

When biscuits are removed from the oven, brush with melted butter and serve hot with jam/preserves or syrups.

When baking biscuits, judge by smell and color than strictly following a suggested time limit. They will begin to smell "nutty" when they are at peak. Also, the bottoms will be golden and the tops just start showing color.

Sausage Gravy for Biscuits

1 lb. pork sausage
1/3 cup flour
2 cups milk or half and half, more as needed
Salt and pepper, to taste

Brown the sausage over medium heat in a large skillet, breaking it into small pieces as it cooks. When the sausage is cooked throughout, sprinkle the flour over the meat and stir to coat. Cook for a couple of minutes until the flour is soaked into the meat.

Pour in half of the milk and stir as the gravy thickens. Pour in the remainder of the milk and stir until it comes to the consistency you like. If it gets too thick, add additional milk as necessary. Add salt and pepper to taste and serve over biscuits, breakfast potatoes, or eggs.

Beer Biscuits

Beer biscuits are great served with sausage gravy, jams, and jellies or alongside any meal.

2 cups all-purpose flour
3 teaspoons baking powder
½ teaspoon salt
1/8 cup shortening
1/8 cup butter, frozen
¾ cup beer, room temperature
2 tablespoons sugar

Preheat oven to 400 degrees. Sift together flour, baking powder, sugar and salt. Grate butter over flour mixture and cut in shortening, using a fork or knife. Stir in beer. Roll out to ¾" thickness and cut with a 2" biscuit cutter. Bake 12 to 15 minutes or until lightly browned.

When biscuits are removed from the oven, brush with melted butter.

Bebe's Blueberry Biscuits

Bebe's Blueberry Biscuits

2 cups all-purpose flour
1 cup milk or half and half
1/3 cup sugar
5 tablespoons unsalted butter, frozen
4 teaspoons baking powder
½ teaspoon salt
3 ounces blueberries (fresh or dried)

Freeze butter for at least 30 minutes. Preheat oven to 425 degrees. Mix salt, sugar, flour and baking powder in a bowl and sift. Grate frozen butter and incorporate into the flour mixture. Add the blueberries and toss lightly. Carefully add the cold milk and using a fork, mix until just combined.

Fold dough and knead slightly and pat into a circle about ½" to ¾" thick. Cut with a 2" biscuit cutter. Place on an ungreased cookie sheet or cake pan.

Place in oven and bake for about 9-10 minutes or until lightly golden. Melt 1 tablespoon of butter and brush over the biscuits when they are removed from the oven.

Glaze:

1 cup powdered sugar
1/8 cup of water
1 teaspoon vanilla
½ teaspoon lemon juice - adjust this to match your taste
¼ teaspoon lemon zest

Allow the biscuits to cool 5 minutes while you mix the glaze ingredients. Once slightly cooled, drizzle the glaze over the biscuits and step aside as your family storms the area!

Strawberries in a Biscuit

½ cup butter, frozen
2 ½ cups self-rising flour
1/3 cup sugar
¼ teaspoon baking powder
1 cup chilled heavy cream
1 cup fresh, chopped strawberries
2 tablespoons melted butter

Preheat oven to 425 degrees. Mix dry ingredients. Grate butter over dry ingredients and use a fork to incorporate. Add strawberries and toss lightly to combine. Pour in cream and combine.

Knead 3 or 4 times and pat into a 1" thick circle. Use a 2" biscuit cutter and place on a cookie sheet or cake pan.

Bake for 15 minutes or until the biscuits are lightly browned. Brush with melted butter.

Cheddar Biscuits

1 cup whole wheat baking mix (like Hodgson Mills)
1/3 cup milk or half and half
1 tablespoon tarragon
½ cup cheddar cheese, shredded
1 ½ tablespoons butter, melted
1/8 teaspoon garlic powder

Preheat oven to 425 degrees. In a large mixing bowl, combine baking mix milk, tarragon and cheese. Place on greased cookie sheet. Bake 20 to 25 minutes or until lightly golden.

In a small bowl, mix melted butter and garlic powder. Brush on biscuits just before serving. My family always loved these with beef stew or chili.

Super Small Super Good Scones

½ cup all-purpose flour
1 tablespoon sugar
½ teaspoon baking powder
1/8 teaspoon baking soda
1/8 teaspoon salt
¼ teaspoon cinnamon
3 ½ tablespoons butter, cold
½ cup oats
¼ cup dried fruit (raisins, currants, dried cherries, or dried cranberries)
¼ cup buttermilk
¼ teaspoon orange zest

Preheat oven to 400 degrees. Sift together all dry ingredients (flour, sugar, baking powder, baking soda, salt, cinnamon and orange zest). Add oats and dried fruit to the flour mixture.

Grate butter over flour mixture and use a fork to incorporate. Pour buttermilk over mixture and stir lightly to just combine. Pat out in a ¾" thick circle and cut into 4 or 6 wedges. Bake for 15 minutes or until fragrant.

Serve with butter and jam. This is a great recipe for morning coffee or if you only need a few scones. You can easily double the recipe if more scones are needed.

Pretty as a Peach Scones

2 cups all-purpose flour
½ teaspoons salt
¼ cup sugar
½ teaspoon cinnamon
1 tablespoon baking powder
6 tablespoons cold butter
2 large eggs
1/3 cup plain Greek yogurt
½ teaspoon almond extract
½ teaspoon vanilla extract
1 cup diced peaches

Preheat oven to 375 degrees. Lightly grease a baking sheet or line with parchment paper.

In a large bowl, whisk together flour, salt, sugar, cinnamon and baking powder. Grate butter over flour mixture and use a fork to incorporate.

In a separate bowl, whisk together eggs, yogurt, and flavorings. Stir wet ingredients into flour mixture until combined. Add peaches to mixture. This will be a sticky dough.

Use a ¼ cup measuring cup or muffin scoop to place "blobs" of dough on the cookie sheet. Sprinkle scones with coarse sugar if desired. Bake for 20-25 minutes or until golden.

Vanilla Bean Scones

2 cups all-purpose flour
3 tablespoons sugar
1 tablespoon baking powder
½ teaspoon salt
5 tablespoons butter, cold
1 cup heavy cream
2 vanilla beans, split and scraped
1 teaspoon vanilla extract

    Preheat oven to 450 degrees. Mix dry ingredients (flour, sugar, baking powder, salt, vanilla bean scrapings). Grate cold butter over flour mixture, incorporating with a fork. Add heavy cream and vanilla extract.

    Pat into a ¾" circle and cut into wedges. Place wedges on parchment covered cookie sheet, sprinkle with additional sugar on top if desired and bake 12–15 minutes or until lightly golden on the edges.

Cranberry Orange (or Cherry Almond) Scones

2 cups all-purpose flour
2 tablespoons sugar
2 teaspoons baking powder
¼ cup butter, cold
½ cup heavy cream
1 egg
1 cup dried cranberries
1 to 2 teaspoons orange zest (I use 1 teaspoon for a lighter orange flavor)

    Preheat oven to 425 degrees. In a large mixing bowl, combine dry ingredients (flour, sugar, baking powder, orange zest, dried cranberries). Grate cold butter over the flour mixture and incorporate with a fork. In a small bowl, beat egg lightly and add heavy cream. Pour milk and egg mixture to flour mixture and stir only until just combined.

    Pat into a ¾" thick circle and cut into wedges. Sprinkle with coarse sugar (or additional granulated sugar) and bake for 15 minutes.

Pumpkin Scones with Maple Ginger Glaze

2 ¼ cups of self-rising flour
½ cup of firmly packed dark brown sugar
1 ½ teaspoons pumpkin pie spice (I am allergic to Nutmeg, so I used 1 teaspoon cinnamon, ¼ teaspoon ground cloves, and ¼ teaspoon ground ginger)
½ cup cold butter cut in small pieces (or grate frozen butter)
2/3 cup canned pumpkin
3 tablespoons whole milk (or half and half)
1 large egg
1/3 cup toasted pecans

Preheat oven to 375 degrees. In a large bowl, combine flour, brown sugar and pumpkin pie spice. Using a pastry cutter, cut in butter until mixture appears crumbly. In a small bowl, whisk together pumpkin, milk, and egg. Add pumpkin mixture to flour mixture, stirring until all combined.

Turn dough onto a floured surface. Knead gently 3 or 4 times. Put dough on a baking sheet lined with parchment paper and pat into an 8" circle. Lightly cut into 8 wedges. Bake until golden brown. Test with a wooden pick inserted in the center. It's done when it comes out clean. The scones will most likely need to bake for about 20 minutes. Let completely cool on a wire rack. Drizzle with **Maple-Ginger Glaze**. Sprinkle with pecans. *garnish with crystallized ginger if desired.

Maple-Ginger Glaze

1 cup confectioner's sugar
5 teaspoons whole milk or half and half
1/8 teaspoon ground ginger
1/8 teaspoon maple extract

In a medium bowl combine confectioner's sugar, milk, ginger and maple extract. Stir to form a thin glaze. Use immediately.

These scones are great with coffee as a breakfast bread OR leave off the glaze and put the pecans in the dough for a savory scone to serve with soups.

Easy Peasy Blueberry Muffins

1 ½ cups all-purpose flour
¾ cup granulated sugar plus 1 tablespoon for muffin tops
½ teaspoon salt
2 teaspoons baking powder
1/3 cup canola or vegetable oil
1 large egg
1/3 - ½ cup milk (read directions below)
1 ½ teaspoons vanilla extract
1 cup of fresh blueberries

Preheat oven to 400 degrees. Line muffin cups with paper liners and spray lightly with non-stick cooking spray.

Whisk together the flour, sugar, baking powder, and salt in a large bowl. Add oil to a measuring cup that holds at least one cup. Add the egg, then fill the cup to 1 cup line with milk. Add vanilla and whisk to combine.

Add milk mixture to the bowl containing the flour mixture, using a fork to combine. Do not overmix. The muffin batter will be quite thick. Add the blueberries and stir carefully to combine. Fill muffin cups 2/3 full.

Sprinkle a little sugar on each muffin and bake for 15-20 minutes or until tops are no longer wet. Transfer to a cooling rack.

Add a little lemon zest for additional flavor. This basic batter can be used with different berries, including strawberries, blackberries, or raspberries. Taste the batter and adjust sugar/flavorings as necessary.

Just Peachy Muffins

Topping:
¼ cup sugar
¼ teaspoon cinnamon
1/8 teaspoon ground ginger

>Preheat oven to 400 degrees

>In a small bowl, mix the topping ingredients and set aside.

Muffins:
1 ½ cups all-purpose flour
¾ cup sugar
2 teaspoons baking powder
½ teaspoon ground ginger
1 teaspoon cinnamon
½ teaspoon salt
1/3 cup vegetable oil
1 large egg
1/3 - ½ cup milk or half and half
1 ½ teaspoons vanilla extract
½ teaspoon almond extract
1 ¼ cups chopped peaches (leave the skin on!)
Optional: cupcake liners

You will need to grease or line muffin cups in a muffin tin. Whisk together the flour, sugar, baking powder, ginger, cinnamon, and salt until well combined. Toss in the peaches and coat with the flour mixture. In a measuring cup, combine vegetable oil, egg and then add milk to make a total of 1 cup liquid. Add vanilla and almond extracts after measurement. Add wet ingredients to dry, stirring just to combine.

Fill muffin cups 2/3 full and sprinkle with the topping mixture. Bake 15-20 minutes or until tops are golden brown. Let cool in the pan for 5 minutes before moving to a wire rack to cool slightly before serving.

Pecan Pie Muffins

1 cup chopped pecans, mixed with 1 tablespoon melted butter
1/2 cup all-purpose flour
1 cup firmly packed brown sugar
2 large eggs, lightly beaten
8 tablespoons (1-stick) unsalted butter, melted
¼ teaspoon salt

Preheat oven to 300 degrees. Spread the buttered pecans on a baking sheet covered with parchment paper and toast nuts in the oven for 4 to 6 minutes, or until fragrant. Remove from oven and allow to cool slightly.

Increase the oven temperature to 350 degrees. Line 6 cup muffin tin with paper liners and spray lightly with non-stick cooking spray.

Combine the toasted pecans, flour and brown sugar in a large mixing bowl. Make a well in the center of the dry ingredients; add the eggs and melted butter and mix just until the dry ingredients are moistened.

Spoon the batter into the paper-lined muffin cups, filling ¾ full. Bake for 20-25 minutes, or until the tops are lightly browned. Remove from the pan immediately to a wire rack and let cool for 5-10 minutes. Serve warm with breakfast or afternoon tea.

Gingerbread Muffins

2 cups all-purpose flour, sifted
½ teaspoon baking soda
2 teaspoons baking powder
½ cup sugar
½ teaspoon ground cloves
2 eggs, lightly beaten
½ teaspoon cinnamon
2/3 cup milk or half and half
1/3 cup shortening (or butter), melt whichever you use
2/3 cup molasses or cane syrup
Optional: ½ cup raisins

Either spray a muffin tin with non-stick cooking spray or line cups with paper liners and spray lightly with cooking spray.

Preheat oven to 350 degrees. Sift dry ingredients together in a large mixing bowl. *(optional: add raisins to the dry mix).* In another bowl, combine eggs, milk, syrup and melted shortening/butter.

Add the egg mixture to the dry ingredients, stirring only until just combined. Bake muffins for 18 to 20 minutes. Your house will smell like Christmas as they bake. I like to sprinkle these with coarse sugar to add an extra crunchy texture.

Biscuit Cinnamon Rolls

Biscuit Cinnamon Rolls

Biscuit Dough:
2 cups all-purpose flour
4 teaspoons baking powder
½ teaspoon salt
1 teaspoon sugar
5 tablespoons cold butter
1 cup buttermilk

Filling:
¼ cup melted butter
½ cup firmly packed light brown sugar
1 teaspoon cinnamon

Glaze:
1 cup powdered sugar
½ teaspoon vanilla extract
2 tablespoons melted butter
2-3 tablespoons heavy cream (start with 2 and increase if glaze is too thick)

Preheat oven to 450 degrees. Cut a parchment round and place in the bottom of a 9" round baking pan. Spray parchment paper with non-stick cooking spray.

In a small bowl, mix the light brown sugar and cinnamon and set aside for filling. In a large mixing bowl, combine flour, baking powder, salt and sugar. Grate cold butter and toss in flour mixture to mix. Make a well in the center of the flour mixture and put in buttermilk. Using a fork, mix dough together until all dry ingredients are moistened. Roll dough into a 1/3" thick rectangle.

Brush dough rectangle with melted butter (1/4 cup) and sprinkle with cinnamon sugar mixture. Roll the dough into a log and cut into 1" thick slices. Place rolls in pan and bake 15 minutes. Allow rolls to cool for about 5 minutes while the glaze is being prepared. In a small bowl, mix powdered sugar, vanilla, butter and heavy cream until smooth and desired consistency. Serve warm or room temperature. Best if eaten the same day they are made. I like to sprinkle toasted pecans over icing and sometimes add 1/3 cup of raisins to the filling.

Sweet Potato Apple Walnut Muffins

1 ¾ cups all-purpose flour
1 ½ teaspoons baking powder
1 teaspoon cinnamon
3 tablespoons canola oil
¾ cup firmly packed light brown sugar
2 eggs, lightly beaten
½ cup whole milk or half and half
1/3 cup chopped walnuts
1/3 cup golden raisins
1 ¾ cups peeled, chopped apples
15 oz. can sweet potatoes, drained and mashed or 1 cup fresh sweet potatoes, cooked and mashed. (A 15 oz. can with syrup will have roughly 8 oz. of sweet potatoes once the syrup is drained off.)

Preheat oven to 400 degrees. In a bowl combine the flour, baking powder and cinnamon, set aside. In another bowl, combine the oil, brown sugar, eggs and mashed sweet potatoes and milk. Make a well in the center of the dry ingredients and add the sweet potato mixture, stirring until moistened.

Fold in the apples, walnuts and raisins. Spoon batter into paper-lined or coated muffin tins. Fill each muffin cup ¾ full. Bake for 20 to 25 minutes or until lightly browned. This recipe makes about 18 muffins and is a great treat to take to work or any family gathering.

Breakfast Sweet Bread

1 cup sugar
2 cups all-purpose flour
1 tablespoon baking powder
½ teaspoon salt
1 egg, lightly beaten
1 cup milk or half and half
1/3 cup vegetable oil
Optional ingredients are listed below for the variations on this base recipe

Spray a loaf pan with non-stick cooking spray. Preheat oven to 350 degrees.

Combine sugar, flour, baking powder, and salt. Beat together egg, milk and oil. Gradually add the dry mixture to the wet until just moist. Add any optional ingredients (see below) at this point.

Pour batter into prepared loaf pan and sprinkle with coarse sugar or granulated sugar for an added crunch. Bake 50 minutes.

Cranberry Orange Bread: add ½ cup dried cranberries, ½ teaspoon orange zest and a squirt of orange juice.

Blueberry Almond Bread: add ¼ cup blueberries and ¼ cup sliced almonds.

Lemon Tea Bread

½ cup butter (1-stick), room temperature
1 cup sugar
2 eggs, lightly beaten
½ cup milk or half and half
1 ½ cups all-purpose flour
1 teaspoon baking powder
½ teaspoon salt
1 lemon, zested and juiced (divided)
½ cup sugar (for drizzle)

Preheat oven to 350 degrees. Either grease or use non-stick cooking spray to prepare a loaf pan.

Cream butter, 1 cup sugar, eggs and zest from lemon. Beat well to combine. Add dry ingredients alternately with milk. Bake in greased loaf pan for 50 minutes to 1 hour or until lightly golden on top. In a small bowl, mix the juice of the lemon with the ½ cup sugar. Drizzle over bread as soon as it comes out of the oven.

This is one of those recipes that has ingredients you typically always have on hand in your kitchen. Make this loaf as an after-school snack or just a sweet treat for your family. The loaf freezes well, although our family never had leftovers to freeze unless I doubled the recipe, serving one, and freezing the other.

This bread is great served with raspberries, blackberries or blueberries.

Harvest Apple Bread

1 ½ cups all-purpose flour
1 teaspoon cinnamon
½ teaspoon baking soda
¼ teaspoon baking powder
¼ teaspoon salt
1/8 cup vegetable oil
1/8 cup butter, melted
1 cup sugar
1 egg, lightly beaten
¼ teaspoon vanilla extract
1 cup peeled, chopped apples
½ cup nuts (pecans, walnuts)

Preheat oven to 350 degrees. Spray a loaf pan with non-stick cooking spray and set aside.

In a large mixing bowl, combine flour, cinnamon, baking soda, baking powder, and salt until combined. Set aside.

In another bowl, combine oil, melted butter, sugar, and eggs, vanilla and apples. Add flour mixture and stir only until combined. Pour batter in the prepared loaf pan and bake for 40 to 45 minutes or until bread is browned. Test with a wooden pick, if it's clean, then it's done. You should see few crumbs and no wet batter.

Allow bread to cool for about 5 to 10 minutes, then remove from loaf pan to cool on a wire rack until ready to serve. This bread smells and tastes like Fall. It is also yummy any other time of the year!

Nanner Bread

(easy Banana Bread recipe)

1 1/3 cups sugar
½ cup butter, softened to room temperature
2 eggs
½ cup buttermilk
1 teaspoon baking soda
1 teaspoon baking powder
2 cups all-purpose flour
1 teaspoon vanilla extract
1 ¼ cups mashed bananas
¾ cup chopped pecans

Preheat oven to 300 degrees. Spray a loaf pan with non-stick cooking spray and set aside.

Cream sugar and butter together until smooth. Add eggs, one at a time, mixing well after each addition. Stir baking soda into buttermilk and add to mixture.

In a mixing bowl, sift baking powder with flour and blend into creamed mixture. Add vanilla extract, then mashed banana and pecans. Pour into prepared loaf pan and bake for 60 minutes or up to 1 hour and 15 minutes or until golden and tests done with wooden pick.

OR use 4 mini-loaf pans and cook for 50 to 60 minutes.

Tropical Banana Bread

1 ½ cups all-purpose flour
1 cup sugar
½ teaspoon baking soda
1/2 teaspoon salt
2 large eggs, lightly beaten
1 teaspoon vanilla extract
¾ cup vegetable oil
1 cup mashed ripe bananas
8 oz. crushed pineapple, drained
½ cup chopped nuts

Preheat oven to 350 degrees. Coat loaf pan with non-stick cooking spray and set aside.

In a large mixing bowl, combine flour, sugar, baking soda, and salt. In a separate bowl, combine eggs, vanilla, vegetable oil, banana and pineapple. Mix wet ingredients with dry and pour into the prepared loaf pan. Bake for 50 minutes, then test with wooden pick. Cool in pan for 10 minutes before removing to a wire rack. This bread stays so moist and is a frequent request from friends and family alike.

Cranberry Artisan Bread

1 cup plus 6 tablespoons warm water
2 ½ teaspoons yeast
1 ½ teaspoons salt
1/8 cup sugar
1/8 cup olive oil
3 ¼ cups all-purpose flour
½ cup chopped pecans or walnuts
¾ cup dried cranberries

Preheat oven to 450 degrees. Mix flour, yeast, salt, sugar, nuts and cranberries. In a separate bowl, mix warm water and olive oil and pour into flour mixture, mixing with a wooden spoon. Leave the dough in the bowl and cover with a tea towel. Allow the dough to rise for an hour or two. Put extra flour on counter or on parchment paper. Dump the dough onto a floured surface. Form into a round loaf and cover with a tea towel and let rise for another hour.

Place a lidded, greased Dutch oven into preheated oven and warm for 10 to 15 minutes. Carefully remove pot from oven and put bread round in the middle of the Dutch oven, cover with the lid and return to the oven to bake for 20 minutes. Remove cover and bake until lightly browned on top (additional 5 to 10 minutes). Cool for an hour before slicing and serving with butter.

Small Soda Bread

2 cups flour
¼ cup oats
2 tablespoons sugar
½ teaspoon baking soda
½ teaspoon salt
¼ cup butter, melted
¾ cup buttermilk
½ cup currants or raisins
Orange zest (about ¼ to ½ teaspoon)

Preheat oven to 375 degrees. Place parchment paper on a baking sheet and set aside. Whisk together the flour, oats, sugar, baking soda and salt in a large bowl. Make a well in the center of the flour mixture and add melted butter and buttermilk. Stir gently until dough comes together. Fold in currants/raisins and zest.

Turn onto a floured surface and knead gently for about a minute. Dough will be sticky. Pat into a 6" circle on the prepared parchment covered baking sheet. Slash a large X (½" deep) across the center of the top. Bake for 25 minutes.

Yeast Rolls

1 cup plus 2 tablespoons warm water
1/3 cup vegetable oil
2 tablespoons active dry yeast
¼ cup sugar
1 teaspoon salt
1 large egg, lightly beaten
3 ½ cups bread flour (use all-purpose if you don't have bread flour)

Preheat oven to 400 degrees. Using a stand mixer, combine the water, oil, yeast and sugar and allow it to rest for about 15 minutes. Using your dough hook, mix in the salt, egg and flour.

Knead with hook until well incorporated and dough is soft and smooth. It should just take a few minutes for the dough to start to pull away from the hook.

Form dough into 12 balls, uniform in size, and then place in a greased 13 x 9" pan and allow to rest for another 10 minutes. Bake for 10 minutes or until golden brown. Serve warm with lots of butter.

Cornbread

6 tablespoons unsalted butter, melted (plus butter for greasing the baking dish)
1 cup cornmeal
¾ cup all-purpose flour
1 tablespoon sugar (leave out if using cornbread for dressing)
1 ½ teaspoons baking powder
½ teaspoon baking soda
¼ teaspoon salt
2 large eggs, lightly beaten
1 ½ cups buttermilk

Preheat oven to 425 degrees. Lightly grease an 8" cast iron skillet or baking dish. In a large bowl, mix the cornmeal, flour, sugar, baking powder, baking soda, and salt.

In a separate bowl, mix the eggs, buttermilk, and butter. Pour the buttermilk mixture into the cornmeal mixture and combine until there are no dry spots (batter will be lumpy). Pour the batter into the prepared baking dish. Bake until the top is golden brown and tester comes out clean, about 20 to 25 minutes. Remove cornbread from the oven and let it cool for 10 minutes before serving.

Tomato Bread

Tomato Bread

2 ½ cups all-purpose flour
1 tablespoon baking powder
1 teaspoon each (salt, garlic salt, crushed oregano, & sugar)
½ cup grated cheddar cheese
¼ cup grated parmesan cheese
1/3 cup milk
1 (14.5-ounce) can stewed tomatoes with green chilis
2 eggs, lightly beaten
¼ cup vegetable oil
½ small jalapeno, minced

Stir together the first 8 ingredients plus jalapenos (if desired). Drain the liquid from tomatoes into a measuring cup and add enough milk to make 2/3 cup. Add the liquid, eggs, and oil to the dry ingredients and stir to blend. Cut the tomatoes into small chunks and carefully fold into the batter (it will be a stiff batter). Spread into a greased and floured loaf pan and bake at 350 degrees for 50 minutes to 1 hour.

This bread smells like pizza and is a great compliment to any chili or hearty stew.

Sweet Cornbread Cake

½ cup all-purpose flour
½ cup sugar
½ cup white corn meal
1 teaspoon baking powder
Pinch of salt
1 tablespoon Canola Oil
½ cup whole milk
1 egg, lightly beaten

Preheat oven to 400 degrees. Spray a 9" pie pan or cast-iron skillet with non-stick cooking spray and set aside.

Sift flour, sugar, corn meal, baking powder and salt into a medium sized mixing bowl. In another bowl, pour oil and milk. Add lightly beaten egg to milk mixture. Add dry ingredients stir only until combined.

Pour batter into prepared pan and bake for 20-30 minutes or until golden brown

Broccoli Cornbread

2 boxes cornbread mix (like Jiffy)
4 eggs, lightly beaten
1/2 cup (1 stick) +2 tablespoons of butter, melted then cooled
1 cup small curd cottage cheese
1 medium onion, chopped
10 oz frozen chopped broccoli
Salt, Pepper, Garlic Powder to taste.

Preheat oven to 350 degrees. Place 2 tablespoons of butter in a small skillet to melt. When melted, sauté onion until translucent, add broccoli and set aside.

Combine all ingredients and place in a greased 13 x 9" pan. Smooth with a wooden spoon and bake for 35 minutes or until golden brown on top.

Jalapeno Cornbread Muffins

1 cup all-purpose flour
1 cup yellow corn meal
½ teaspoon baking soda
½ teaspoon salt
1 cup buttermilk
½ cup unsalted butter, melted
1/3 cup sugar
2 large eggs, beaten lightly
1 tablespoon honey
2 small jalapenos, minced
¼ cup shredded cheddar cheese

Preheat oven to 375 degrees. Spray a 12-cup muffin tin with non-stick cooking spray and set aside.

Combine flour, corn meal, baking soda, and salt. In a separate bowl, combine the buttermilk, butter, sugar, eggs and honey. Pour milk mixture into flour mixture, stirring to combine. Add jalapenos, cheese, then pour batter into muffin tin (2/3 full) and bake for 15 to 17 minutes or until tops are golden.

When the muffins are removed from the oven, melt a tablespoon of butter and a teaspoon of honey in the microwave and brush over each muffin. Serve warm.

Mexican Cornbread

1 cup corn meal
2 tablespoons sugar
2 tablespoons all-purpose flour
1 teaspoon salt
½ teaspoon baking soda
1 cup buttermilk
2 large eggs, lightly beaten
1 small can cream style corn
¼ cup bacon grease
1 medium onion, chopped
2 or 3 small jalapenos, minced
1 cup grated cheddar cheese

Preheat oven to 350 degrees. Spray an 8" cast iron skillet with non-stick cooking spray. Heat for 5 to 10 minutes.

Mix corn meal, sugar, all-purpose flour, salt, baking soda, and minced jalapenos. Stir to combine. Add remaining ingredients except the cheddar cheese.

Pour half the batter into the skillet, sprinkle with cheddar cheese and cover with the remaining batter. Bake at 350 degrees for 35 to 45 minutes or until golden and tests clean with a wooden pick.

Never Fail Popovers

4 large eggs, room temperature
1 ½ cups milk
¾ teaspoon salt
1 ½ cups all-purpose flour
3 tablespoons melted butter.

Preheat the oven to 450 degrees and move oven rack to a low position. Grease the popover pan thoroughly inside each cup as well as around the edges.

Pre-heat the popover pan for about 10 minutes while you prepare the batter.

Beat together eggs, milk and salt until combined. Add flour and whisk until the mixture is frothy and all large lumps are gone. Stir in melted butter.

Divide the batter between the pre-heated popover cups. They should be approximately ¾ full.

Bake popovers for 20 minutes and then reduce the heat to 350 degrees and bake for another 10 to 15 minutes. The popovers will be golden brown.

Note: when popovers are removed from the oven, remove from pan and make a small slit in the side to release steam so that popovers will not "fall" or deflate.

Beer Bread

3 cups self-rising flour
¼ cup sugar
1 can beer, room temperature
2 tablespoons butter, melted
1 egg, lightly beaten

Preheat oven to 350 degrees. Spray a loaf pan with non-stick cooking spray and set aside.

In a large mixing bowl, mix flour and sugar until combined. Add beer and mix until blended. Pour into greased loaf pan. Combine egg and butter and brush over top of loaf. Let rise 10 minutes before baking for 340 minutes.

Serve warm with butter. Tastes delicious with beef stew.

Garlic Cheese Toast

10 oz. loaf French bread
¼ cup unsalted butter, softened
¼ cup shredded parmesan cheese
½ cup shredded mozzarella cheese
½ teaspoon minced garlic

Mix butter, cheeses, and garlic together, stirring to combine. Slice French bread into 1" thick slices and spread garlic cheese generously over each slice. Broil just until cheese melts and toast is slightly browned.

This garlic toast is wonderful with baked ziti or spaghetti with meatballs. Freezes well.

Night before Christmas French Toast

10 oz. loaf French Bread from bakery/grocery
8 large eggs, lightly beaten
3 cups milk or half and half
4 teaspoons sugar
½ teaspoon salt
1 tablespoon vanilla extract
3 tablespoons butter (plus extra to grease baking dish)

Butter a 13 x 9" baking pan. Cut bread into 1" thick slices, arrange in one layer in the pan. In a mixing bowl, combine milk, sugar, salt and vanilla, mix thoroughly. Pour egg mixture over, cover and refrigerate overnight. To bake, preheat oven to 350 degrees. Uncover pan and dot with 3 tablespoons butter. Bake for 35-45 minutes or until puffy and browned. Let stand 5 minutes before serving with hot flavored syrups.

This dish is easy to prepare and always receives rave reviews from everyone who tries it. Serve it with homemade syrups, fresh fruit, sausage, or bacon.

Grand Marnier French Toast

6 eggs, lightly beaten
1 cup milk or half and half
2 tablespoons Grand Marnier
1 tablespoon granulated sugar
¼ teaspoon salt
½ teaspoon vanilla extract
4 tablespoons butter, melted and cooled
10 oz. loaf French bread or Challah, sliced 1" thick

In a medium sized mixing bowl, add eggs, milk, Grand Marnier, sugar, salt, vanilla extract and melted butter. When all ingredients are combined, dip each slice of bread, coating all sides completely and fry in butter until browned. Serve with Syrup and fresh fruit.

Granny's Pancakes

3 cups all-purpose flour
½ teaspoon salt
1 tablespoon baking powder
¼ cup sugar
2 large eggs, lightly beaten
½ teaspoon vanilla extract
1 ½ cups milk or half and half
¾ stick of butter, melted

Mix flour, salt, baking powder, and sugar until combined. Add eggs, vanilla, milk and then melted butter. Beat with mixer until smooth.

Cook on griddle over medium to medium high heat. Watch pancakes and when bubbles appear, turn over and cook until golden. Serve with maple or fruit syrup.

This batter will remain fresh for up to a week, if refrigerated.

Honey Baked Pancake

4 eggs, lightly beaten
½ teaspoon salt
¼ cup honey
2 ½ cups whole milk
1 cup all-purpose flour
2 tablespoons butter

Preheat oven to 425 degrees and pace a 10" cast iron skillet in the oven to heat for 10 minutes. Add butter to skillet and return to oven until the butter is melted and hot.

Beat eggs, honey, salt and milk. Add flour gradually until smooth. When butter in skillet has melted, add the batter quickly and return skillet to the oven to bake for 25 to 30 minutes or until the center is like custard. Cool for 5 minutes. Cut and serve with powdered sugar, honey, berries, peaches or strawberries.

Weekend Baked Apple Pancake

2 large apples, sliced
4 tablespoons sugar, divided
1 teaspoon cinnamon
½ teaspoon ground ginger
1/3 cup unsalted butter
1/3 cup dark brown sugar
¾ cup all-purpose flour
½ teaspoon salt
1 cup whole milk
½ teaspoon vanilla extract
5 large eggs, lightly beaten
Powdered sugar (optional)

Preheat oven to 400 degrees. Peel, core and slice apples. You should have approximately 3 cups of sliced apples. Spray a 10" cast iron skillet with non-stick cooking spray and set aside. In a small bowl, mix 3 tablespoons of sugar with cinnamon and ginger and set aside.

Cut butter into uniform pieces and place in the cast iron skillet. Put skillet in the oven to melt the butter as the oven heats. Sprinkle 1/3 cup brown sugar over melted butter. Spread apples on top of brown sugar and sprinkle with sugar, ginger mixture. Return skillet to oven to caramelize the apples while the batter is being prepared.

In a mixing bowl, whisk flour, remaining sugar, and salt. Gradually add milk, then vanilla and eggs. Let batter rest for 5 minutes. Remove the skillet from the oven and pour batter over apples. Bake for 20 minutes. Cool for 5 minutes and sprinkle with powdered sugar if desired.

Serve hot with maple or fruit syrup, fresh fruit, and sausage or bacon.

Blueberry Croissant Breakfast Puff

Each slice is like eating a Danish from a fancy bakery!

3 large pre-made croissants (bakery or grocery), chopped into ¾" pieces
1 cup fresh blueberries (*or optional ingredients list below*)

Custard:
8 oz. cream cheese, softened
1 cup milk or half and half
2/3 cups sugar
2 eggs, room temperature then lightly beaten
1 teaspoon vanilla

Preheat oven to 350 degrees. Coat an 8"x 8" square pan with nonstick cooking spray and set aside. Cut the croissants into ¾ inch pieces and place in the bottom of the baking dish. Sprinkle blueberries over croissants.

Mix custard ingredients and pour over the croissants and blueberries. Make sure all pieces are submerged, soaking up custard.

Bake for 30-35 minutes or until the top is golden brown. Allow to cool for 10 minutes and sprinkle with powdered sugar or serve plain.

This can easily be doubled and made in a 9x13 casserole dish for a crowd.

Almost any berry or fruit will work. Adjust your sugar based on the level of natural sugar in the fruit. Here are some suggestions for tasty alternatives:

***Peaches**; sprinkle in a little **cinnamon**.

***Strawberries**; use **½ teaspoon vanilla and ½ teaspoon almond extracts**. Sprinkle with sliced almonds.

***Blackberries**; sprinkle with a tiny bit of **orange zest** and mix with custard before pouring over berries and croissants.

Apple Cinnamon Baked Oatmeal

1 ½ cups peeled, chopped apples
4 tablespoons brown sugar; divided
2 teaspoons cinnamon; divided
1 cup old fashioned rolled oats
½ teaspoon baking powder
¼ teaspoon salt
1 cup milk
1 egg
3 tablespoons unsalted butter; melted
1 teaspoon vanilla

Preheat oven to 350 degrees. Butter or spray an 8" x 8" baking pan and set aside to layer ingredients.

Layer One: In a large bowl, add chopped apple, one tablespoon brown sugar, and one teaspoon cinnamon. Toss and put in greased baking pan.

Layer Two: In the same bowl, combine oats, one teaspoon cinnamon, baking powder and salt. Stir together and sprinkle over fruit.

Layer Three: In the same bowl, whisk together milk, egg, remaining three tablespoons brown sugar, butter and vanilla. Pour over oats, coating evenly. Bake for 30 minutes.

**Serve with fruit, nuts, and whipping cream. Pour the whipping cream around a square of the baked oatmeal and sprinkle nuts and fruit over the top. Also, great "plain".

Note: You can easily double this recipe and bake in a 13 x 9" baking pan. Lasts about 3 days in the refrigerator. Simply cut a square of the oatmeal and microwave for about 15-20 seconds for breakfast each morning.

Chocolate Banana Oatmeal Cups

1 ½ cups old fashioned oats (also called rolled oats)
¼ teaspoon ground cinnamon
½ teaspoon baking powder
1/8 teaspoon salt
1 egg
1/8 cup maple syrup
½ cup mashed banana (approximately 1 banana)
1 teaspoon vanilla extract
½ cup milk
1/8 cup melted coconut or vegetable oil
½ cup mini chocolate chips

Preheat oven to 350 degrees. Mix dry ingredients. Mix wet ingredients. Mix wet ingredients with dry. Slowly stir in chocolate chips. Spray muffin pan or use paper muffin liners. Bake for 30 minutes.

Wrap individually in plastic wrap and then freezer bag. If frozen, heat for two minutes. Put a coffee mug of water in the microwave to keep muffins from drying out.

Oven Omelet

¼ cup butter
1 ½ dozen eggs, lightly beaten
1 cup plain Greek yogurt
1 cup milk
1 to 1 ½ teaspoons salt (use 1 teaspoon and adjust as needed)
¼ cup chopped green onions, tops and bottoms

Heat oven to 325 degrees. Spray a 13 x 9" baking dish with non-stick cooking spray. Then put butter in baking dish and heat to melt, tilt and coat the entire bottom of the dish.

In a large mixing bowl, beat eggs, yogurt, milk and salt until blended; stir in onions. Pour mixture into dish and bake until eggs are set, but still moist, about 35 minutes.

If you have fewer people to serve, half the ingredients and use an 8" x 8" square baking pan. Cook for 30 minutes, check to see if eggs are set but still moist. If not yet set, return to oven for another 5 minutes.

Max's Green Chili Casserole

(great for breakfast or as a side dish)

5 large eggs, lightly beaten
½ pint cottage cheese
¼ cup butter, melted
¼ cup all-purpose flour
½ cup shredded Monterrey Jack Cheese
½ teaspoon baking powder
¼ teaspoon salt
4 oz. diced green chilis
½ cup shredded cheddar cheese

Preheat oven to 350 degrees. Beat eggs and add remaining ingredients. Bake in buttered 8" x 8" baking dish. Bake for 35 minutes or until eggs are set.

You could easily add in 1/3 cup chopped ham (if so, reduce the salt) or 1/3 cup browned sausage, chopped, prior to baking for a heartier breakfast.

Breakfast Casserole

1 lb. pork sausage
3 to 4 bakery croissants or bread slices, cut into small cubes
1 cup shredded cheddar cheese
9 large eggs, lightly beaten
3 cups whole milk
1 ½ teaspoons dry mustard
¾ teaspoon salt
1/8 teaspoon black pepper

Spray a 13 x 9" pan with non-stick cooking spray and set aside.

Brown sausage in a medium skillet, stirring to crumble. Drain well and set aside. Arrange bread cubes in bottom of greased baking dish. Top with cooked sausage and sprinkle with cheese.

In a medium mixing bowl, whisk together eggs and next 4 ingredients; pour evenly over cheese. Cover and chill 8 hours. These steps can easily be handled the night before, making it a perfect holiday morning breakfast or weekend brunch.

Let the dish stand at room temperature for 30 minutes while preheating the oven at 350 degrees. Bake for 45 minutes or until eggs are set.

Hearty Sweet Potato Hash

1 large or 2 small sweet potatoes, chopped into bite-sized pieces.
½ cup red or orange bell pepper, chopped
2 handfuls of baby spinach
1 large tomato, chopped
1 ½ teaspoons olive oil
2 cloves of garlic, crushed
2 chicken sausages, chopped and cooked (I like chicken/apple but works with chicken, turkey or pork sausage).
4 to 5 pieces bacon, cooked and chopped
Salt and pepper, to taste
Sprinkle of cayenne pepper (no more than a pinch)

In a large, cast iron skillet, sauté oil and garlic for 1 minute. Add chopped sweet potato and stir.

Cook potatoes for 4 to 5 minutes before adding the peppers, onions, and tomatoes. Sauté for 5 minutes, stirring occasionally.

Mix in cooked sausage and bacon and cook another 5 to 7 minutes, stir often after adding the cooked meats.

Mix in fresh spinach and cook 2 to 3 minutes.

Remove from skillet and serve hot with your choice of eggs, bread and fruit. I typically plate individually and top with their choice of cooked egg.

Mediterranean Quiche

½ teaspoon olive oil
1 teaspoon minced garlic
3 cups (packed) fresh baby spinach
4 to 5 eggs, lightly beaten
1 cup whole milk (or half and half or heavy cream)
½ cup sun dried tomatoes, drained and chopped
4 ounces goat cheese
Pie crust for 9" pie
Salt and pepper, to taste

Prepare pie crust, put in 9" pie pan and refrigerate until ready to fill. Preheat oven to 350 degrees.

Heat olive oil and garlic in a medium skillet over medium heat. When garlic becomes fragrant, add the spinach and allow to wilt slightly, about 2 minutes.

Pre-bake crust for 8 minutes. Add wilted spinach to crust and smooth layer. Sprinkle sun dried tomatoes over spinach then add crumbled goat cheese.

In a mixing bowl, stir together the eggs and milk, season with salt and pepper, pour egg mixture evenly over ingredients. Bake for 45-55 minutes, or until the eggs are set and top of quiche is lightly browned.

Ham and Swiss Strata

3 large bakery croissants, cubed in small pieces
8 ounces chopped cooked ham
1 ½ cups shredded Swiss cheese
6 large eggs, lightly beaten
1 cup half and half
1 tablespoon honey
½ teaspoon dry mustard or 1 teaspoon spicy brown mustard
½ teaspoon salt
¼ teaspoon black pepper
Fresh parsley for garnish

Spray a deep-dish pie plate or 8" x 8" baking pan with non-stick cooking spray. Place cubes of croissants in baking pan in an even layer. Sprinkle with cooked ham, then top that layer with cheese.

In a medium mixing bowl, lightly beat eggs, half and half, honey, mustard, salt and pepper until well combined. Evenly distribute egg mixture over layers and cover with foil. For a more intense flavor, refrigerate 8 hours or overnight. If you do not have time for that, simply baked after combining, the result will still be delicious.

Preheat oven to 325 degrees. Bake, covered, for 35 minutes. Uncover and bake another 20-30 minutes longer or until a knife inserted in the center comes out clean.

Let the casserole stand for 10 minutes before serving. Serve large squares garnished with fresh chopped parsley, for an extra pop of color. Great served with fruit to round out a hearty breakfast.

Breakfast Sausage

1 lb. ground pork
1 teaspoon fennel seed
1/2 teaspoon minced garlic
1 teaspoon paprika
½ teaspoon black pepper
½ teaspoon sage
½ teaspoon salt
2 tablespoons coconut or canola oil
¼ teaspoon cayenne pepper or use red pepper flakes
¼ teaspoon white pepper

Combine pork, garlic and all spices, mix until fully combined. Form into 2" round patties (this recipe makes approximately 8 patties).

Heat skillet with 1 tablespoon coconut oil per 4 patties. Cook 3 to 4 minutes per side or until there is no pink when you cut into the center of a sausage.

Easy Breakfast Potatoes

2 large russet potatoes scrubbed and pricked with a fork in several places.
1 to 2 tablespoons olive oil for frying
1 teaspoon dried parsley
1 small sprig fresh rosemary
Salt and pepper, to taste

Put the whole, scrubbed, pricked potatoes into the microwave for about 3 minutes (depending on size). This allows the cooking process to start but is not meant to fully cook the potatoes which will be hot and hard when removed. Allow the potatoes to cool slightly.

In a large skillet, heat the olive oil over medium-high heat. Leave skin on and cube potatoes.

Chop rosemary leaves. Add potatoes, rosemary, parsley, salt and pepper to the oil, toss and fry on medium-high heat, covered, for about 10 to 15 minutes, tossing periodically.

When cooked, remove lid so they brown for 5 to 10 minutes. Serve hot

.

Among the Texas Bluebonnets

Chapter Five

The Main Event

In the small East Texas town of Mineola, Texas, population 4,686 according to the 2017 census, stood a stately mansion known as the Noble Manor. Named for Dr. Samuel Cloud Noble, a prominent citizen of the community, the house was an American Foursquare that boasted nineteen rooms and a dining room the size of a small football field.

The home's construction started in 1910 and was completed three years later. The house had elaborate crown molding throughout and hardwood floors that once restored, shined gloriously. At over 7,500 square feet, there was ample room for four adults and a lively teenager.

Our teenager populated the third floor where a fully finished out ballroom had been built by the original owner. The walls were a fine polished wood and a bathroom had been installed, making it an island for my beautiful girl. There were several nooks and crannies where said teenager stored hundreds of pairs of flip flops and enough clothes to establish a retail store.

Many fond memories were formed in that lovely house. Slumber parties, holidays with extended family and friends and a constant flow of teenagers to keep life interesting. Food seemed to be at the center of the time spent in the house.

One of my favorite memories was when my son Max brought his best friend, Ben. We had so much fun cooking together, spending time, and hanging out. The time spent with Max and Ben was so special, I think often of the many memories of my children, their friends and our family gatherings. Their laughter echoed throughout the house and stays in my heart.

The house had a portico that we used to display the old model A that belonged to my sweet mother-in-law's husband, Loyal. Loyal was a WWII veteran who was trained to cook for the soldiers. He was amazing in the kitchen, even into his 90's. He could make rolls that were perfectly formed, and he always used all of the dough, nothing was wasted. How they came out so perfect, every time, is a mystery. He also could fry a catfish better than almost anyone I knew. He made his own cornmeal batter and served his catfish with the lightest hush puppies you've ever tasted. Loyal loved any meal and always enjoyed company. He was very entertaining and had hundreds of stories to share.

When the weather was still just slightly warm, in early Spring one year, Byron and I invited over about six people for barbecue and conversation. We intended to grill outside and then eat inside the dining room. Both Byron and I made trips to the grocery store, he to get meat to grill and I to get ingredients for several side dishes and desserts. While at the grocery store, I ran into some folks who said that they had heard we were cooking out with friends. I promptly invited them to bring a side and told them what time to be there. Byron also ran into several people and invited them as well.

By the time we both got home, the telephone had been ringing and even more guests were coming. Our intimate dinner for six turned into a blowout barbecue for over thirty people. Welcome to Texas. There were several trips to the grocery store to make sure we had enough food for the crowd.

By far one of the most enjoyable barbecues we've put together. Byron grilled several selections of meat perfectly, making the entire neighborhood smell amazing, while I laid out potato salad, baked beans, and other sides as well as homemade brownies, ice cream, my fudge sauce, and a couple of peach cobblers. Every time I looked at Byron, beside the grill, there was a group of men discussing grilling, making suggestions or just standing there talking and drinking a beer or iced tea.

Instead of focusing on table dressing and using china, we opted for paper, plasticware and served buffet style to allow us to spend time with our friends. We used 6-foot tables covered in red gingham and lawn chairs to seat everyone. There was great conversation with bursts of laughter and folks had such a nice time.

The moral to this story is that IF you would like an intimate dinner party for six, don't go to the grocery store and if you must, never make eye contact or answer the phone, if you live in a small town.

Byron and I wish every party or get together would have the same result: A large group of friends, sitting outside enjoying the warm Texas sun and helping themselves to mounds of Texas favorites!

Chicken Fried Steak with Gravy

Chicken Fried Steak

4 cube steaks (about 1/3 lb. each
1 ½ cups all-purpose flour
2 teaspoons fresh ground black pepper, divided
2 teaspoons kosher or sea salt, divided
½ teaspoon smoked paprika
½ teaspoon onion powder
½ teaspoon garlic powder
½ teaspoon baking soda
½ teaspoon baking powder
1 ½ cups buttermilk
2 teaspoons Tabasco (or your favorite hot sauce)
2 eggs
1 cup vegetable oil

In a shallow bowl or pan, whisk together flour, one teaspoon black pepper, one teaspoon salt, paprika, onion powder, garlic powder, baking soda and baking powder. Set aside.

In a separate bowl, whisk together buttermilk, hot sauce, and eggs. Set aside.

Dry cube steaks with a paper towel, removing as much moisture as possible. Season meat with remaining teaspoon of salt and pepper. Let meat sit for 5 minutes and pat dry again with paper towel. Dredge the cube steaks in the flour mixture, shaking off excess, then dredge in buttermilk-egg mixture, letting excess drip off, and then once again in the flour mixture, shaking off excess.

Place breaded cube steaks on a sheet pan or metal rack and press any of the remaining flour mixture into the cube stakes, making sure the entire steak is covered. No need to deep-fry steaks, simply add the cup of vegetable oil to make at least ¼" deep.

Test the oil by dropping a bit of breading into the pan of oil. The breading should sizzle. If you prefer to use a thermometer, the temperature should be between 320 to 340 degrees. Fry 2 steaks at a time, 3 to 4 minutes each side or until golden brown. If you flip the steaks or crowd them in the pan, the breading will fall off.

Remove the steaks from pan and drain on paper towels. Place in a pre-heated oven to keep warm until serving. Great served with baked mashed potatoes, green beans and rolls.

Gravy

4 tablespoons grease (I use leftover bacon grease)
4 tablespoons flour
2 to 3 cups whole milk
½ cup heavy cream
Salt and pepper, to taste

Mix grease and flour in a cast iron skillet over medium heat, stirring until smooth. Add milk and cream, stirring constantly until it thickens to gravy consistency. Add salt and pepper according to your taste.

*When serving chicken fried steak, I heap the steaks on a large platter and serve gravy in a gravy boat. Everyone has their own thoughts about steak to gravy ratio.

Bowl of Red aka Texas Chili

(No beans!)

Weekends are for complicated chili recipes that take all day to prepare and simmer. In contrast, this chili can be a delicious alternative. I make this many times when I am looking for a hearty meal in less than an hour. This chili is thick and very adaptable, based on your preferences. Add fresh chilis (poblanos, jalapenos or any favorite), serve with accompaniments such as avocado, shredded cheese, onions, black olives, corn chips or hot sauce so that your family or guests can "doctor it up" as they wish. I typically make the cornbread cake to go alongside as it is a little buttery and sweet. It tends to reduce the heat if you happen to add too much hot pepper to your chili and need something to cool your flame!

1 ½ to 2 pounds ground beef
1 large yellow onion, diced
1 large green pepper, diced
2 small or 1 large jalapenos, minced
¼ cup tomato paste
15 ounce can diced tomatoes
2 cups beef broth (low sodium)
2 ½ tablespoons chili powder
1 ½ teaspoon cumin
¾ teaspoon salt
1/8 cup corn starch
Hot sauce, 4 or 5 dashes, or to taste

Add the ground beef, onion, and bell pepper to a large Dutch oven and cook over medium heat, breaking up the meat as it cooks. When the meat is fully cooked, drain all the fat from the pan.

Add the jalapeno, garlic, tomato paste, diced tomatoes, beef broth, chili powder, cumin and salt and stir. Bring to a boil and reduce heat to a simmer. In a very small bowl, mix the corn starch with a small amount of the chili, stir to ensure no lumps remain. Pour the mixture into the chili and stir to combine. Simmer chili for at least 20 minutes but will be better if you simmer for about an hour, stirring occasionally. Add hot sauce to taste. Serve with sour cream and shredded cheddar cheese.

Tacos al Carbon

1 (4 ½-pound) beef brisket, trimmed
2 tablespoons brown sugar
1 ½ teaspoons ancho chili powder
½ teaspoon garlic powder
½ teaspoon onion powder
½ teaspoon chopped parsley
½ teaspoon salt
¼ teaspoon black pepper
Flour or mixed tortillas
Toppings: shredded cheese, sour cream, chopped tomatoes, salsa, guacamole, and shredded lettuce

Preheat the oven to 300 degrees. Place brisket, fat side down, in a roasting pan. In a mixing bowl, combine brown sugar, powders, parsley, salt and pepper. Rub spice mixture into top of brisket. Cover and seal pan with foil. Bake for 4 ½ hours.

Remove the brisket from pan and let stand for 15 minutes. Cut brisket across the grain into thin slices, using a sharp knife. Serve in warm tortillas with desired toppings.

Baked Ziti

1 ½ pounds ground beef or ground sirloin
2 spicy Italian sausages
1 large jar of traditional spaghetti sauce (your favorite)
2 cups water
1 cup part-skim ricotta cheese
1/8 cup shredded parmesan
12 oz. package of Ziti or Rigatoni
¾ cup part-skim mozzarella cheese, shredded

Preheat oven to 400 degrees. Spray 13" x 9" baking dish with nonstick cooking spray and set aside. Brown beef and sausage and set aside. In a large bowl, combine sauce and water. Stir in beef, ricotta and other cheeses, and last incorporate uncooked pasta.

Pour into a 13x9 baking dish. Cover with foil and bake 55 minutes. Remove foil and sprinkle with additional mozzarella. Bake uncovered for another 5 minutes or until bubbly and cheese is melted.

Serve with salad and garlic cheese toast.

Mom's Goulash

2 pounds ground beef or ground sirloin
1 large can of tomatoes, with juice
1 small or medium onion, chopped
1 tomato can full of water
1 teaspoon salt
¼ teaspoon pepper (or more to taste)
5 to 6 dashes of pepper sauce (Tabasco or your favorite hot sauce)
1 to 1 ½ cups macaroni

Brown meat with chopped onion in Dutch oven or stew pot over medium heat. Once the meat mixture is lightly browned, add salt and pepper. Pour off any excess grease. Add macaroni, tomatoes, water and pepper sauce. Simmer 20 to 30 minutes.

Feel free to add corn, green beans or other vegetables to enhance the flavor. If you are adding, I would use a cup of corn or green beans. This recipe is easily doubled or tripled to feed a crowd. This hearty meal is great served with cornbread and a small salad.

Beef Empanadas

2 ¼ cups all-purpose flour, spooned and leveled, plus more for your work surface.
Kosher salt and freshly ground pepper, to taste
½ cup (1-stick) cold unsalted butter, cut into pieces
1 tablespoon cider vinegar
5 large eggs, divided
2 tablespoons olive oil
½ poblano chile, seeded and diced
1/3 cup fresh corn kernels
¼ yellow onion, diced
1 plum tomato, seeded and diced
1 garlic clove, minced
½ pound ground beef
1 ½ teaspoons tomato paste
1 tablespoon plus 1 teaspoon minced fresh oregano
1 teaspoon salt
20 brine-cured green olives, pitted and chopped
Canola oil, for frying

Whisk together flour and 1 teaspoon salt in a bowl. Cut butter into flour mixture with two forks or a pastry blender until mixture is fine and grainy. Whisk together vinegar, one egg and 1/3 cup ice water in a bowl. Pour egg mixture into flour mixture and stir with a wooden spoon until dough comes together in a rough mass.

Turn dough out onto a lightly floured surface and knead until smooth, *taking care not to handle excessively*. Form dough into a thick disk, wrap in plastic wrap and refrigerate for an hour.

Boil 3 eggs, peel and chop. Heat olive oil in a large skillet over medium-high heat. Add Chile, corn, onion, tomato and garlic. Sauté until fragrant, 2 to 4 minutes. Add beef and sauté, breaking up meat as it cooks. Once meat is browned, stir in tomato paste and oregano. Season with salt and pepper. Lower heat to medium-low and stir in olives and chopped hard-boiled eggs. Cool mixture for 30 minutes.

Unwrap dough and place on a lightly floured surface; allow to rest for 15 minutes. Roll dough to 1/8" thick. Using a 5 to 6" round cutter, cut out as many rounds as possible. Set rounds aside, gather dough scraps, re-roll to 1/8" thick. Cut remaining rounds from dough.

Whisk together remaining egg and 2 tablespoons water in a bowl. Brush edge of a dough round with egg wash. Place ¼ to 1/3 cup of filling in center of round, fold dough over filling to make a half-moon and crimp edges together tightly with a fork to seal securely. Repeat with remaining rounds.

Heat 3 inches of canola oil in a medium saucepan to 350 degrees. Gently lower empanadas, no more than 3 or 4 at a time, and fry until golden brown. This should take 4 to 6 minutes. Remove to a paper towel-lined plate to drain. Serve hot.

Granny's Perfect Pot Roast

1 teaspoon seasoned salt
½ teaspoon onion powder
¼ teaspoon black pepper
1/8 teaspoon garlic powder
1 (3 to 4-pound) beef chuck roast
1 tablespoon olive oil
¾ cup water or low sodium beef stock
1 large onion, chopped
¼ cup chopped green pepper
2 garlic cloves, minced
2 bay leaves
2 teaspoons dried parsley
¼ teaspoon dried thyme
All-purpose flour

    Preheat oven to 325 degrees. In a small bowl, combine first four ingredients and rub onto roast. In skillet, brown roast in oil, on all sides. Place roast in a roasting pan. Add water or beef stock, onion, green pepper and seasonings. Cover and bake for 2 ½ to 3 hours. Remove from oven, remove roast from pan and place on a serving platter. Cover the roast with foil to keep warm. Discard bay leaves and skim fat from pan juices.

    Measure juices and return to roasting pan. For each cup of juice, combine 1 tablespoon flour with 2 tablespoons water and mix well. Stir flour mixture into pan and cook over medium heat, stirring constantly until thickened and bubbly. Pour a small amount of gravy over roast to keep moist. Serve the remaining gravy in a boat alongside the roast. Great served with popovers and roasted vegetables.

Beef Tenderloin with Champagne Mustard Sauce

Beef-Tenderloin
½ cup red wine vinegar
¼ cup vegetable oil
½ teaspoon salt
½ teaspoon pepper
½ teaspoon dried thyme
1 (5 to 6-pound) tenderloin

Champagne Mustard Sauce
1 tablespoon minced shallot
1 tablespoon vegetable oil
½ cup dry champagne
2 tablespoons butter, softened
2 tablespoons all-purpose flour
1 cup half and half
1 tablespoon Dijon Mustard

In a small bowl, combine first 5 ingredients to make the marinade. Place tenderloin in a shallow dish. Pour marinade over meat and cover tightly with foil. Refrigerate 8 hours (I make the night before the day I will serve). Place rack in roasting pan. Insert a meat thermometer. Bake in a 425 degree, preheated, oven for 45 minutes or until thermometer registers 140 degrees (for rare), basting occasionally with marinade. Bake to 150 degrees for medium rare or 160 degrees for medium. Slice 1/2" slices or thicker and drizzle with champagne sauce.

To prepare champagne mustard sauce, sauté shallots in oil; add champagne. Bring to a boil and cook until liquid is reduced to ¼ cup. Strain liquid, discarding shallots, and set aside. Melt butter in a heavy saucepan over low heat and add flour, stirring constantly. Gradually add half and half. Cook over medium heat until mixture is thick and bubbly. Stir in mustard and reduced champagne mix. Arrange the meat slices on a platter and pour a small amount of sauce down the middle of the slices. Serve the remaining sauce in a gravy boat.

Beef Stroganoff

I have a confession to make: I <u>never</u> fix beef stroganoff. My husband has perfected the dish and my contribution is a side dish or rolls. I found this recipe long ago, but Byron has modified it into one of the most delicious Stroganoffs I've ever tasted.

8 oz. sour cream
3 tablespoons no salt added tomato paste
1 teaspoon Worcestershire sauce
½ cup all-purpose flour
¾ teaspoon salt
1/8 teaspoon fresh ground pepper
2 lbs. tenderloin or sirloin steak, cut into 2 " strips
1 tablespoon butter
½ cup chopped onion
14 oz. low sodium beef broth
2 cups sliced fresh mushrooms (Cremini or button)
8 cups cooked medium egg noodles (7 cups uncooked)
Optional: chopped fresh parsley

Combine the sour cream, tomato paste and Worcestershire sauce in a mixing bowl. Set aside.

Lightly spoon flour into a dry ½ cup measurement cup; level with a knife. Combine flour, salt, and pepper in a large zip-top plastic bag. Add beef; seal and shake to coat each strip.

Melt butter in a large nonstick skillet over medium-high heat. Add onion to pan; sauté 2 minutes or until tender. Add beef and flour mixture to pan; sauté 3 minutes or until the beef is browned. Gradually add broth, scraping pan to loosen browned bits. Add mushrooms; cover and cook 5 minutes or until mushrooms are tender. Reduce heat to low; gradually stir in sour cream mixture. Cook, uncovered. 1 minutes or until heated throughout. Stir in parsley, if desired. Serve over egg noodles.

Apricot Chicken

8 chicken thighs, with bones and skin
Olive oil for browning
Cooked rice

Apricot Sauce:
¾ cup apricot jam or preserves
1 tablespoon soy sauce
Lemon, zest and juice (need at least 2 to 3 tablespoons juice)
Chili flakes (pinch)
Salt and pepper to taste
2 to 3 tablespoons water to thin sauce as necessary

Heat a large, deep frying pan over medium-high heat. Add a splash of oil and brown the chicken pieces on all sides until the skin is crispy and golden, about 10 to 15 minutes.

In a mixing bowl, combine the sauce ingredients. Add 2 tablespoons water to thin the sauce. When the chicken is golden brown and almost cooked through, pour off the excess fat. Return the pot to the heat and add the sauce.

Allow the sauce to simmer gently, basting the chicken regularly until the glaze had reduced and the chicken is cooked through. Serve the chicken with cooked rice.

Sharon's Chicken Tacos/Flautas

My sister-in-law is an excellent cook and shares recipes that are made with wholesome ingredients. She tends to lean toward a healthier lifestyle and her recipes are flavorful and easy to prepare. She has shared several wonderful recipes with me through the years and I know that if I get one of her recipes, serve it to friends or family, I will be sharing the recipe more than once. These chicken tacos are a fast meal and can be served in tortillas as tacos or rolled/fried and served as flautas.

Either way, serve them with bowls of accompaniments like shredded cheese, onions, black olives, lettuce, tomatoes, etc. When I make as flautas, I drain most of the juice from the taco meat before rolling in a cylinder to fry. Flautas scream for guacamole, salsa, and possibly a little sour cream.

2 pounds chicken thighs, with bone
1 can diced tomatoes with green chilis (like Rotel)
1 can stewed tomatoes
1 medium onion, chopped
1 teaspoon chili powder
½ teaspoon cumin
Sprinkle or two of paprika
Sprinkle of oregano
Corn tortillas

Using a small amount of oil, brown chicken in frying pan over medium heat. Add chopped onion, spices, canned tomatoes and continue to cook over low medium heat. Continue to simmer in sauce until chicken is done and tender.

Remove chicken from sauce and pull meat from the bone. Return the chicken to sauce and simmer without lid to enable the sauce to thicken and reduce.

When the chicken mixture is fully cooked and heated through, place a small amount of chicken mixture in the center of each corn tortilla and garnish as a taco and serve or **roll chicken mixture in tortilla and fry to make flautas.** Serve with cheese, Pico de Gallo and guacamole.

White Chicken Chili

You'll notice the name of this chili doesn't include "Texas". Well, as Texans know, there are NEVER any beans in Texas Chili. However, whether this might be considered "Yankee Chili" or not, you will absolutely love the taste and texture of this chili. The chili is mild so plan to adjust to your personal heat level. The texture is creamy and full of vegetables, beans, and chicken. Give this wonderful chili a try but please don't tell them you got the recipe from a Texas Belle. I have my reputation to uphold.

3 boneless/skinless chicken breast
1 ½ teaspoons ground cumin
1 ½ teaspoons ground coriander
1 teaspoon dried oregano
¼ teaspoon paprika
¼ teaspoon red pepper flakes
1 cup dried Great Northern Beans (soak overnight, drain, and add to crockpot)
2 stalks celery, chopped
1 clove garlic, minced
4 oz. chopped green chilis
1 medium onion, chopped
1 bell pepper, chopped
½ to 1 jalapeno, minced with seeds removed
2 cups chicken broth (low sodium)
½ cup whole milk
1/8 cup cornstarch
¾ cup fresh or frozen corn
Juice of ½ lime
¼ cup Monterey jack, shredded

Mix all ingredients except for milk and cornstarch. Cook in slow cooker or crockpot for 7.5 hours. Mix milk and cornstarch in liquid measuring cup, stirring until fully combined. Pour cornstarch mixture into crockpot and cook chili until thickened or about 30 minutes more.

Chicken Alfredo Casserole

12 ounces Ziti or Rigatoni
2 cups shredded cooked chicken
1 ½ cups shredded Mozzarella cheese

Alfredo Sauce:
1 tablespoon olive oil
4 cloves garlic, minced
3 tablespoons all-purpose flour
1 cup low sodium chicken broth
1 cup milk or half and half
¾ cup freshly grated parmesan cheese
½ teaspoon salt
¼ teaspoon black pepper

Preheat oven to 375 degrees. Spray a 13 x 9" baking pan with non-stick cooking spray and set aside. Cook pasta according to package directions. Drain and toss with Alfredo Sauce.

For Alfredo sauce, heat olive oil in a large skillet, add garlic and sauté 1 minute. Sprinkle in flour, stir another minute. Slowly add all chicken broth. Stir in milk, parmesan, salt and pepper.

Layer half of the pasta with Alfredo sauce in the bottom of the baking pan. Top with 1 cup of cheese then layer second half of pasta. Top with remaining ½ cup of cheese. Bake for 20-25 minutes or until bubbly and heated through. Serve hot with garlic toast and salad.

Chicken Pot Pie

1 tablespoon bacon drippings
1 tablespoon olive oil
1 tablespoon butter
½ teaspoon minced garlic
1 onion, chopped
2 carrots, chopped
1 potato, chopped
½ pound mushrooms, sliced
¼ teaspoon salt or to taste
¼ teaspoon black pepper or to taste
1/8 teaspoon cayenne
1/8 teaspoon dried thyme
¾ cup chopped celery
½ cup frozen green peas
¼ cup all-purpose flour
1 cup half and half
2 cups low sodium chicken stock or broth
2 cups chicken, cooked and cubed
1 package puff pastry (thawed)
1 large egg, slightly beaten

Preheat oven to 425 degrees. In a Dutch oven, heat oil, drippings and butter. Stir in onions, carrots, potatoes, celery, mushrooms and all spices. Cook over medium heat for 8 to 10 minutes.

Sprinkle in flour, cook for 2 minutes. Pour in stock and milk. Add cooked chicken and simmer to thicken the sauce. Divide equally among 4 ramekins or 6" skillets. Cut 4 squares of pastry, fold over the top of each dish and slice to vent. Lightly beat the egg and brush over the tops of the pies. Place individual serving dishes on a cookie sheet and bake until bubbly and pastry is golden, approximately 20 to 30 minutes.

Chicken and Dumplings

1 large fryer chicken, with liver/gizzards/neck removed
1 large onion, peeled and cut in quarters
3 carrots, peeled and cut into large pieces
3 stalks of celery, cut into large pieces
Salt and Pepper to taste
Dumplings
3 cups all-purpose flour
¾ teaspoon baking soda
¾ teaspoon salt
4 ½ tablespoons shortening (or half butter and half shortening)
1 cup milk

Place the chicken, onions, carrots, and celery in a large stock pot and cover with water. Bring to a boil, then reduce heat so water maintains a gentle simmer. Allow chicken to simmer until cooked through – approximately an hour.

Mix flour, baking soda, and salt together in a mixing bowl. Cut in shortening/butter, using two knives or your fingertips until the mixture resembles small peas. Add milk, a ¼ cup at a time until biscuit dough consistency. You may not need the entire cup of milk listed above.

Stir until a ball of dough just begins to form. On a floured surface, roll dough to about ¼" thick. Using a pizza cutter or sharp knife, cut the dough into strips approximately 1" wide by 2"es long. Place the strips on a floured baking sheet and refrigerate for 30 minutes so that the dumplings maintain their shape in the broth.

When chicken is done, remove from the broth and let cool. Remove all chicken from bones and shred into bite-size pieces. Discard the bones, skin and liver/gizzards/neck. Pour broth through a fine mesh strainer and discard all vegetables. Reserve 6 cups of the broth for the dumplings. If you have more than 6 cups, be sure to freeze the remaining broth for use in another recipe.

In a large pot, over medium-low heat, bring broth to a gentle simmer and drop in dumplings, a few at a time. Cover the pot and allow to simmer for 10 minutes. Reduce heat to low and add back the chicken. Allow to simmer until thickened or about 20 minutes. Season with salt and pepper to taste.

Chicken Skewers with Thai Peanut Sauce

Skewers:
1-pound chicken tenders, breast meat
Olive oil
Wooden skewers
Salt and pepper, to taste

Sauce:
½ cup creamy peanut butter
1/3 cup low sodium soy sauce
¼ cup cilantro leaves
3 tablespoons rice wine vinegar
3 tablespoons lime juice
3 tablespoons honey
3 tablespoons sesame oil
1 teaspoon Dijon mustard

Soak wooden skewers in a pan of water for at least 30 minutes or until you are ready to assemble. Thread one or more breast strips on each wooden skewer. Brush each side of the chicken with olive oil, then salt and pepper both sides lightly and grill over medium heat for 6 to 8 minutes, turning once. Serve hot or at room temperature with Thai Peanut Sauce.

In a food processor, combine all the sauce ingredients and process until smooth. Pour sauce into a gravy boat and serve alongside the platter of chicken skewers. The sauce is rich, so we like to serve skewers, steamed rice and sauce for a tasty meal.

Chicken Pecan Fettuccine

3 tablespoons butter
3 tablespoons flour
½ cup chicken broth
½ cup half and half
1/8 teaspoon cayenne
1-pound boneless chicken breasts
Salt and pepper according to your taste
¼ cup chopped pecans
1 package fettucine

Boil fettucine according to package directions; drain and set aside. Cut chicken into bite-sized pieces. Put chicken in a saucepan and cover with water. Boil chicken until done.

In a large cast iron skillet, melt butter and add flour to make a light roux. Stir together over medium heat until flour smells nutty or approximately 3 minutes. Add chicken stock and half and half, stirring over medium heat until thickened. Add salt and pepper, cayenne, pecans and cooked chicken, stir to combine. Serve over fettucine with a tossed salad.

Sour Cream Chicken Enchiladas

1 lb. roasted chicken
1 cup shredded white cheese
12 tortillas
cooking oil to sauté the tortillas

Sauce

¼ cup butter
¼ cup flour
2 cups chicken broth
1 cup Greek yogurt or sour cream
4 oz. can diced green chilis, drained

Preheat oven to 350 degrees. Spray a 13 x 9" baking pan with non-stick cooking spray and set aside.

Remove chicken from bone and set aside to cool. In a medium skillet, put a small amount of oil and fry tortillas slightly to make them more pliable. Each side of the tortilla should be less than a minute. Drain on paper towels. This process makes the tortillas more pliable when forming the enchiladas.

Make sauce in a medium saucepan over medium-low heat. Put butter and flour in the saucepan and stir until a very light brown roux is achieved. Add chicken broth and stir to combine. Add 1 cup Greek yogurt and diced green chilis. Simmer for 5 minutes or until all the flavors combine.

Put a small amount of sauce in the bottom of the 13 x 9" baking dish. Take one of the tortillas, place about 2 teaspoons of chicken, 2 teaspoons of cheese in the center of the tortilla and roll tightly. Put in the baking dish, seam down, and repeat until all enchiladas are rolled.

Pour the sauce over the enchiladas, just enough to cover each one, sprinkle top with additional cheese and bake for 20 to 30 minutes or until bubbly and heated through. Any leftover sauce can be served in a gravy boat to top off the enchiladas at the table.

King Ranch Chicken

(Mom's version)

¼ cup unsalted butter
1 medium green bell pepper, chopped
1 medium onion, chopped
1 can condensed cream of mushroom soup
1 can condensed cream of chicken soup
10 oz. can of tomatoes with green chilis drained (I use Rotel "hot")
2 cups cooked chicken
12 corn tortillas, cut into strips
2 cups shredded cheddar cheese

Preheat oven to 325 degrees. In a large saucepan or skillet, melt butter over medium heat. Add bell pepper and onion and sauté until tender. Add soups, tomatoes, cooked chicken and stir to combine. Simmer for 5 to 10 minutes then remove from heat to cool slightly.

Layer half of the tortilla strips in bottom of a greased 13 x 9" baking dish. Pour half of the chicken mixture over the tortillas and sprinkle with half of the shredded cheese. Repeat another layer, ending with the remainder of the shredded cheese on top. Bake uncovered for 40 minutes or until heated through.

Crock Pot Tetrazzini

1 bunch green onions, tops and bottoms
1 small jar pimento, chopped into small pieces
¼ to ½ cup shredded cheese (cheddar or mozzarella)
1 cup chopped celery
1 green bell pepper, chopped
½ lb. fresh mushrooms, sliced
3 cups cooked chicken, turkey or ham, cubed
1 tablespoon fresh chopped parsley
1 cup each (broth, water, and milk)
8 oz. spaghetti, broken
1 tablespoon olive oil
Salt and pepper, to taste

Cook, rinse and drain spaghetti, according to package directions. In a large skillet, add oil and cook onions, bell pepper and celery 1 to 2 minutes with all seasonings including salt and pepper.

Layer ingredients in crock pot in the following order; Meat, vegetables (except mushrooms), spaghetti, mushrooms and pimento. Sprinkle with cheese, cover with lid and cook on low for 7 to 8 hours.

Tequila-Lime Chicken Drumsticks

¾ cup silver tequila
¾ cup freshly squeezed lime juice (6-8 limes)
1/3 cup honey
1 tablespoon plus 1 ½ teaspoons coarse salt
¾ teaspoon freshly ground black pepper
4 ½ pounds chicken drumsticks (about 20)
3 tablespoons canola oil
Clementine or orange wedges, for serving (optional)

Combine tequila, lime juice, honey, salt, pepper, chicken and oil in a large Ziploc bag (gallon size). Place in a 13 x 9" baking dish and let stand at room temperature, turning the bag occasionally for 1 hour.

Preheat oven to 375 degrees. Remove chicken from marinade, allowing excess to drip back into the bag. Pat dry. Reserve the marinade. Place chicken on a parchment-lined rimmed baking sheet. Bake until cooked through and golden brown, about 40 minutes.

Transfer marinade to a saucepan and boil over medium-high heat until thickened and reduced by half. This should take about 15 to 20 minutes. Transfer chicken to a serving platter and immediately brush with glaze. Can be served warm or room temperature, with clementine wedges.

Garlic and Citrus Roast Chicken

2 tablespoons soy sauce (low sodium)
3 tablespoons honey
2 tablespoons minced fresh thyme
1 orange, zested and juiced
1 lemon, zested and juiced
1 lime, zested and juiced
2 cups low-sodium chicken broth
8 garlic cloves, unpeeled
1 onion, quartered
1 roasting chicken (5-pound)
1 tablespoon lemon-pepper seasoning

Heat oven to 375 degrees. In a mixing bowl, combine first 3 ingredients and juices from each fruit. Add broth, garlic and onions to roasting pan. Place chicken on a rack in the pan; season with lemon-pepper seasoning. Roast 1 ¾ hours or until done, basting with citrus mixture after 30 minutes and again 30 minutes later. Transfer chicken to platter. Cover; let rest 20 minutes. Skim fat from pan juices.

Peel garlic and mash into juices. Place a saucepan on the stove over medium heat; add remaining citrus mixture. Bring to a boil, scraping up brown bits. Stir in citrus zest. Reduce heat and simmer until thickened. Season with salt and pepper. Serve sauce in gravy boat, alongside chicken.

Chicken Piccata

4 boneless, skinless chicken breast halves (about 6 oz. each)
Salt and pepper
Flour for dredging
4 to 5 tablespoons olive oil
4 tablespoons butter
2 lemons (1 thinly sliced, 1 juiced)
4 cloves garlic, finely minced
3 tablespoons capers, rinsed and drained
½ cup dry white wine
¼ cup finely chopped parsley

Split and butterfly the chicken. Starting on the fat side of the chicken breast, cut horizontally across the breast but not all the way through. Open it up like a book. Pound the chicken to 1/4" thickness.

Place a serving platter or large plate in the oven and preheat to 250 degrees.

Heat a large skillet over medium to medium-high. Season the chicken with salt and pepper and dredge in flour, shaking off the excess. Pour 1 or 2 tablespoons olive oil into the preheated skillet. Working in batches, brown the chicken lightly on each side, adding additional oil as necessary. Transfer cooked chicken to the warmed platter, cover with foil and keep warm while you make the lemon-butter sauce.

Melt the butter into the chicken drippings. Add the lemon slices and lightly brown. Add the garlic and stir 1 minute. Add the capers. Deglaze the pan with the wine and add the lemon juice and parsley. Slide the chicken back into the pan and coat with the sauce. Return the chicken to the platter and drizzle with the pan sauce. Serve with garlic cheese toast.

Slow Cooker Ribs

1 rack of baby back pork ribs
1/4 bottle of your favorite barbecue sauce (I like sweet baby ray's)
12 oz. can of Dr. Pepper
1 ½ tablespoons brown sugar
1 teaspoon garlic salt
½ teaspoon black pepper

Create your rub by mixing all the dry ingredients in a bowl. Cover both sides of the ribs completely with rub and then place bones down in a crock pot or slow cooker. Please the lid on the slow cooker and cook on high for 30 minutes.

Turn the heat down to low. Remove the lid and pour the Dr. Pepper over the ribs, then brush with barbecue sauce. Replace the lid and cook on low for 6 ½ hours.

Preheat the grill or oven to finish at 350 degrees for 8 to 10 minutes to help caramelize the sauce, right before serving.

You may adjust the amount of the barbecue sauce based on your taste. I have always used a smaller amount because my family likes the taste of the ribs and not as much sauce. You can use up to a 28 oz. bottle of sauce if you desire.

Grilled Pork Chops with Wine Sauce

4 to 6 bone in center cut pork chops, 1" thick
¾ cup dry white wine
¼ cup honey
¼ cup plus 1 tablespoon Dijon mustard
2/3 cup heavy cream
¼ teaspoon salt
¼ teaspoon white pepper
1 tablespoon butter

Sear center cut pork chops on high grill heat for about 3 minutes per side to provide beautiful grill marks. Reduce grill to medium heat and cook the pork chops an additional 4-7 minutes, depending on the thickness of the chop. The chops should register 145 degrees on a meat thermometer in the center of the chop to signify properly cooked.

While the meat is grilling, prepare the sauce for the chops. Combine wine, honey, and mustard in a heavy saucepan and bring to a full boil. Lower heat to low medium and cook, stirring occasionally until sauce is reduced by half. Lower heat to simmer and stir in cream. Season with salt and pepper, to taste and simmer another 15 minutes.

When you are ready to serve, remove the sauce from the heat and add in the tablespoon of butter. Line the pork chops on a platter and drizzle a little sauce to keep the meat moist as you serve dinner. The remainder of the sauce should be poured into a gravy boat to serve alongside the meat for anyone who would like additional sauce.

This dish is wonderful with roasted vegetables and baked mashed potatoes.

Parmesan Pork Chops

4 pork chops, boneless about 1" thick
½ teaspoon garlic powder
½ teaspoon black pepper
1 tablespoon olive oil
½ cup Italian breadcrumbs
½ cup parmesan cheese

Preheat oven to 350 degrees. On a plate, combine cheese, breadcrumbs, pepper and garlic powder.

Rub pork chops with olive oil and then coat in cheese mixture. Make sure fully coated, press onto pork if necessary. Line pan with parchment and place rack over parchment paper. Coat rack with nonstick cooking spray. Place pork chops in oven and bake for 40-45 minutes.

Baked Ham with Honey-Mustard Sauce

4-pound fully cooked boneless ham
1 cup apple cider
¼ cup firmly packed dark brown sugar
4 tablespoons country style Dijon mustard
4 tablespoons honey

Preheat oven to 350 degrees. Place ham in the center of a 13 x 9" baking dish. Pour apple cider over ham. In a medium bowl, stir together remaining ingredients and spoon sauce over ham. Bake, basting every 15 minutes, for at least an hour or until heated through.

Ham, Asparagus, & Gruyere Quiche

Ham, Asparagus, & Gruyere Quiche

1 cup of ham steak, cut into small pieces
1 bunch of fresh asparagus, bottoms cut off (baked/chopped)
1 ½ teaspoons Italian leaf parsley, diced fine
½ cup Gruyere cheese
1/8 teaspoon paprika
½ teaspoon salt
1/8 teaspoon black pepper
6 to 8 large eggs, lightly beaten
1/8 cup heavy cream
Unbaked pie shell for 9" pie
1 tablespoon olive oil for roasting asparagus
Sprinkle of salt and pepper for roasting asparagus

Preheat oven to 425 degrees. Use a cookie sheet covered with parchment paper to roast asparagus. Place asparagus on covered sheet and drizzle with olive oil, sprinkle with salt and pepper. Roast for 20 minutes or until cooked through and starting to brown. Remove the asparagus from the oven and set aside to cool.

Put pie dough in pie pan and flute edges. Layer half of the chopped ham, then half of the asparagus, grate cheese over layers and repeat until all ingredients are used. Mix beaten eggs, cream, parsley, paprika, salt and pepper. Pour over layered ingredients and bake for 30 to 35 minutes or until eggs are set and tops starts to brown lightly

Southern Baked Ham

6-pound ham
1 cup molasses
12 oz. can Coca Cola
20 oz. can of sliced pineapple, reserve juice

Preheat oven to 425 degrees. Drain pineapple, set slices aside but reserve juice. Mix pineapple juice, molasses and Coca Cola together. Place ham in the center of a 13 x 9" baking dish. Baste with glaze mixture. Continue to baste every 10 to 15 minutes until the ham is done (about 2 hours). Ham cooks at 18-20 minutes per pound at this temperature. Garnish top of the ham with pineapple slices and brown in the oven.

Mom's Tuna Casserole

2 ½ cups medium egg noodles (measure dry)
1 cup frozen peas
1 can Cream of Celery condensed soup
½ cup milk or half-and-half
6 oz. can tuna, drained and flaked with a fork
1 cup shredded cheddar cheese
Paprika, sprinkle to taste
Salt and pepper, to taste

Preheat oven to 400 degrees. In a large stock pot, cover noodles with water, few shakes of salt and prepare according to package directions. Add peas for last 5 minutes of cooking time. Strain pasta and peas then set aside.

In a 2-quart casserole dish, combine the soup, milk, tuna and half of the cheese. Stir in noodles and peas. Top with remaining cheese and sprinkle with Paprika.

Bake for 20-25 minutes or until bubbling and hot. Serve with salad and hot rolls or cheddar biscuits.

Jumbo Crab Cakes with Chive Aioli

Crab Cakes
1 lb. jumbo lump crabmeat
1 large egg
1 teaspoon Worcestershire sauce
Juice from 1 large lemon
1 cup mayonnaise
1 teaspoon creole mustard
1 tablespoon minced parsley
Finely ground breadcrumbs (for extra richness, use bakery croissants, grind in food processor)
2 tablespoons of butter
Salt and pepper, to taste

Chive Aioli
¼ cup fresh chives
2 garlic cloves, peeled
½ cup water
1 cup mayonnaise
Salt and pepper, to taste

Prepare Aioli and refrigerate. Combine chives, garlic and water in the bowl of a food processor and process until smooth. Stir in mayonnaise, salt and pepper to taste. Place in refrigerator while you prepare crab cakes.

Whisk the egg until frothy, add Worcestershire sauce, lemon juice, mayonnaise, mustard and parsley. Gently fold in the crabmeat. Add just enough breadcrumbs to bind together. Start with 2 tablespoons and add additional until the proper consistency is achieved. Divide mixture into 8 crab cakes. Sauté in butter until golden brown, approximately 2 minutes per side.

Place crab cakes in a warm oven until all are cooked. Serve with Chive Aioli

Shrimp Creole

This recipe came to me from my sister-in-law, Sharon, and was originally obtained by my mother-in-law, from Brennan's Restaurant when they had a Downtown Dallas location.

1 onion, diced
1 green pepper, diced
1 cup celery, chopped
1 garlic clove, minced
1 large can tomatoes
1 small can tomato paste
2 bay leaves
1/8 teaspoon cayenne pepper
½ teaspoon oregano
2 to 3 pounds small to medium shrimp
2 tablespoons corn starch
1/4 cup water

Sauté vegetables until tender. Stir in tomatoes, garlic, bay leaves, cayenne, oregano and salt and pepper. Boil on medium-high heat and then reduce to simmer creole for 30 minutes or more. Add shrimp and cook until pink, probably 4 or 5 minutes. Add tomato paste. Stir to combine.

Combine ¼ cup water and 2 tablespoons of corn starch, stir until combined. Add to the creole and stir. This will serve as a thickener for the sauce. If needed, you can add additional water if creole appears too thick.

Serve over cooked rice.

Cheese Enchiladas with Red Sauce

Make the sauce first, then the enchiladas.

Enchilada Sauce:

4 tablespoons extra virgin olive oil
4 tablespoons flour
4 level tablespoons chili powder
1 teaspoon garlic powder
1 teaspoon onion powder
1 teaspoon cumin
½ teaspoon salt
1/8 teaspoon cayenne pepper
4 cups chicken broth

Heat the oil in a small saucepan over medium/low heat. Add the flour and whisk for a minute. Add all the spices and stir together. Gradually add the broth, whisk to prevent lumps.

Simmer, stirring for 15 minutes or until the sauce starts to thicken. A little of this sauce is tasty and a lot can be overwhelming. This is not chili con carne so don't drown your enchiladas in sauce. Just cover enchiladas with enough sauce to keep them moist.

Use immediately or store in an airtight container (mason jar works well) in the refrigerator for up to a week.

Cheese Enchiladas with tamale, guacamole, refried beans and rice

Cheese Enchiladas with Red Sauce *(cont.)*

Enchiladas:
24 corn tortillas
2 cups white cheddar cheese or regular cheddar; grated
2 cups Monterrey Jack cheese; grated
1 small onion, finely diced (optional)
Corn oil

Preheat the oven to 350 degrees. While enchilada sauce cools slightly, prepare the enchiladas.

Mix cheeses together and set aside. Heat the oil in a skillet over medium heat and when you see small bubbles around the edges of oil, place a tortilla in the hot fat. Immediately turn over and remove to a paper towel lined plate. This process will make the tortillas more pliable. Pat the tops of the tortillas to remove any excess oil. Do this with tortillas to fill a 13 x 9" baking dish. A 13 x 9" pan will hold about a dozen enchiladas.

Put 2 teaspoons of the cheese down the center of the tortilla and roll into a tight enchilada. Put a very small amount of enchilada sauce in the bottom of the baking dish and place enchiladas, seam side down over the sauce. Pour a very light coating of sauce over the enchiladas and sprinkle with any remaining cheese mixture.

Bake in pre-heated oven for 20-30 minutes, or until all cheese is melted and enchiladas have been heated throughout. Serve with refried beans, Mexican rice, guacamole, Pico de Gallo, jalapenos, and chopped onions for a Fiesta of Tex-Mex tastes.

Cowgirl in Training

Chapter Six

On the Side

Although Texas is cattle country, and Texans love their meat, side dishes and vegetables are paramount to the success of a meal. My Daddy came from East Texas and was the son of a farmer/rancher in Houston County. As I've mentioned before, much of my childhood was spent in East Texas, on the ranch, with my grandparents. During spring break, I would help plant beans and other vegetables which my grandfather and uncles would tend until ready to harvest. Acres of fresh vegetables, beans, sweet and white potatoes, etc. were grown there. After harvest, the vegetables that would be separated into those retained and those going to market for sale. Those going to market were sorted, placed in baskets or bins and trucked to the market for sale. The other vegetables and fruits were kept in a cool storage until they were ready for canning.

Following harvest time was always great fun and there was always plenty to do, no talk of boredom by kids in residence. Helping my grandparents can vegetables, or make jams and jellies was a delightful experience that I remember fondly and will always treasure.

When my cousin, Anita, and I were very young we walked into the mudroom and there were many bushel baskets of tomatoes being stored, waiting to be canned. Anita and I found a few tomatoes that were a little squishy and started to squeeze them. That seemed a little fun so we started looking in each basket for the squishy ones, squeezing them and shooting seeds across the floor. One of my cousin's tomato squeezes resulted in tomato seeds across my shirt. Although she absolutely didn't mean to hit me with the juice and seeds, she did laugh as if it was the funniest thing she'd ever seen. Having a firecracker temper at that age, I was furious at her laughter and decided she needed the same experience I'd had. Before we realized how much damage was done, we looked up to see our Papaw standing in the doorway and he wasn't pleased.

We both looked around the room and realized we had been squeezing tomatoes for a while and the floor was covered in juice and seeds, some of the bushel baskets had only half the tomatoes remaining and we looked like we'd been in a major accident as we were covered in red juice.

Needless to say, we spent the remainder of the day cleaning the floor, combining the bushel baskets of tomatoes remaining and taking our second bath of the day. Although it looked like a war zone, we probably only ruined a bushel or maybe a little more of the tomatoes but neither of us got dessert that evening. So, remember to eat your vegetables, don't squeeze them on your cousin, or no dessert for you.

    The vegetables and side dishes in this section are best when made with fresh ingredients, although the recipes can use fresh, frozen or canned vegetables in most instances.

Okra and Tomatoes

14 ½ oz. can crushed tomatoes, undrained
¼ to ½ onion, sliced thin and sautéed in a small amount of butter
½ teaspoon salt
½ teaspoon pepper
1 tablespoon sugar
1 tablespoon butter
1 tablespoon bacon drippings (if you don't keep, use 2 tablespoons butter)
1-pound okra; stemmed and cut into ¼ inch slices (frozen okra works well too)
3-5 dashes of pepper sauce (tabasco, crystal)
1 teaspoon cornstarch (optional)
1 teaspoon water (optional)

In a medium saucepan, combine the tomatoes, onion, salt, pepper, sugar, and melted butter (and bacon drippings if using). Cook over medium heat for 10 minutes. Add the okra and reduce the heat to simmer for an additional 5 minutes.

If the stew isn't thick enough, mix a teaspoon of cornstarch and a teaspoon of water, mixing completely and drizzle into the stewed okra mixture and simmer another 2 to 3 minutes or until it reaches desired thickness.

Serve with peas, cornbread, and roasted chicken.

Fried Okra

My brother-in-law, Craig, makes the best fried okra in the world! He knows that I like at least some of my okra darker brown. He fries okra and leaves a serving in to get dark and crunchy for me. Fried okra, plain, or dipped in cream gravy, is one of my favorite vegetables.

1 lb. Okra (about 10 pods or more), cut in ½" slices
1 egg, lightly beaten
1 cup cornmeal
¼ teaspoon salt
¼ teaspoon black pepper
½ cup vegetable oil
1/8 teaspoon cayenne (less or more to taste)

In a small bowl, soak okra in lightly beaten egg for 5 to 10 minutes. In a medium bowl, combine cornmeal, cayenne, salt and pepper.

Heat the oil in a large skillet over medium-high heat. Dredge okra in the cornmeal mixture, coating evenly. Carefully place okra in hot oil, stir to break apart pieces and move okra around while it cooks. Reduce heat to medium when okra first starts to brown and cook until golden. Drain on paper towels.

Scalloped Potatoes

3 medium potatoes
1 can cream of mushroom soup
1/3 cup milk or half and half
1 cup grated white cheddar (or use ¾ cup white cheddar and ¼ Gruyere)
Salt and pepper, to taste
'1 large onion
Butter for baking dish

    Preheat oven to 350 degrees. Butter a 2-quart baking dish. In a mixing bowl, combine soup, milk, salt and pepper. Slice potatoes thin, with or without skin left on. Slice onions in thin slices. Layer baking dish with potatoes then a layer of onions and ladle on half of the soup mixture. Sprinkle with half of the cheese. Make another layer of each and top with remaining cheese. Bake in a covered dish until the potatoes are tender or about an hour.

Cheesy Grits Casserole

2 cups low sodium chicken broth
2 cups water
1 cup corn grits
4 tablespoons butter,
1 cup shredded cheddar cheese
¼ cup grated parmesan
1/8 teaspoon cayenne
Kosher salt and pepper, to taste
Small amount of shredded cheese to top

Preheat oven to 350 degrees. Grease a small casserole dish and set aside. In a medium saucepan, bring chicken broth and water to a boil and season with salt. Reduce heat to simmer, then whisk in grits. Stir often until grits have absorbed liquid and are tender. This should take about 10 minutes.

Stir in butter and cheeses and cayenne pepper. Taste, and add salt and pepper, to taste. Pour the grits into the greased casserole dish and sprinkle with a small amount of cheese. Bake for 15 to 20 minutes or until the cheese on top is bubbly.

This dish is excellent when served with a big southern breakfast or as a side for dinner.

Black-Eyed Peas

Tradition has it you eat black-eyed peas on New Year's Day for good luck. In Texas and in the South, we eat them year-round.

1 pound dried black-eye peas (washed and drained)
¾ tsp. add more to taste
1/8 cup bacon grease or oil
3 cloves garlic (minced)
1 to 2 green peppers, chopped
1 to 2 onions (chopped)
2 bay leaves
Salt and Pepper to taste
Ham hock or ham steak cut into small chunks
6 splashes of hot sauce (a splash is more than a few drops modify for your comfort)

Wash and pick through peas to find and discard stones. Cover peas with water and soak them overnight. Drain and place in kettle or Dutch Oven and add fresh water to cover. Add ham and salt then start to cook over medium heat.

In a skillet, heat bacon grease or oil, add garlic, green peppers, onions, bay leaves, salt and pepper to taste. When vegetables are tender, remove bay leaves then add the vegetables to the peas and add hot sauce. Cook peas on a low heat until tender roughly 45 minutes to an hour. The longer they cook, the better the flavor. Serve with cornbread and ham slices.

Corn Pudding

Corn pudding is a sweet fluffy way to get our vegetables. It is a cross between a corn souffle and dessert. When my daughter was growing up, she often had friends over for lunch or dinner. Her best friend, Katrina, loved corn pudding and invited herself almost every time she found out I was making it. She also managed to take more home for a later treat. I loved having extended family like Katrina. She is all grown up now, with children of her own. I am so proud we stay in touch through social media.

3 large cans creamed style corn
1 can sweet whole kernel corn, drained
3 large eggs, lightly beaten
4 tablespoons all-purpose flour
½ teaspoon salt
4 tablespoons sugar
4 tablespoons butter
½ cup heavy cream

Heat oven to 350 degrees. Coat a 2-quart baking dish with non-stick cooking spray. Set aside.

In a large bowl, combine the flour, sugar and salt. Add the eggs and mix well. Mix in the cream and melted butter. Whisk with a wire whisk until all combined. Add the drained corn and creamed corn and mix until all combined. Transfer to prepared baking dish. Bake for 1 hour or until edges start to brown and middle is set.

Roasted Parmesan Green Beans

two pounds fresh green beans, washed and drained
four tablespoons olive oil
four tablespoons shredded parmesan cheese
four tablespoons panko breadcrumbs
one teaspoon salt
½ teaspoon garlic powder
one lemon – *optional*

    Preheat oven to 400 degrees. Combine all ingredients in a large mixing bowl; toss to coat. Spread green beans on a parchment lined baking sheet. Roast for 15 to 20 minutes; stirring halfway through. (optional: If you like, squeeze the lemon over after you remove from the oven). Sprinkle with additional parmesan cheese prior to serving.

Roasted Asparagus

Roasted Asparagus

1 pound of fresh asparagus, washed, trimmed
2 tablespoons olive oil
½ teaspoon garlic powder
¼ teaspoon salt
¼ teaspoon black pepper
Juice of ½ lemon

   Preheat oven to 400 degrees. Line a baking sheet with parchment paper. In a mixing bowl, combine olive oil, garlic powder, salt and pepper. Coat the fresh asparagus and place on the baking sheet. Bake for 12 to 20 minutes, depending on the size of the asparagus or until slightly browned and fragrant.

   Remove from oven, drizzle with lemon juice and serve warm.

Byron's Cream Peas

Byron's peas and my cornbread make a nice southern meal.

1-pound fresh cream peas
4 cups water
1 medium onion, chopped
2 strips bacon, chopped in small pieces
ham hock or ham steak with bone (cut in pieces)
¾ teaspoon salt
½ teaspoon black pepper
½ teaspoon chili powder
1 teaspoon cumin
1 clove garlic, minced
1 tablespoon vegetable or canola oil

Put 1 tablespoon oil in Dutch oven or stock pot. Swirl to cover inside bottom of pot. Fry bacon until pliable but not completely cooked. Add chopped onion and cook over medium heat for about 5 minutes. Add minced garlic and cook 1 minute.

Add water to deglaze the pot. Add peas and reduce heat to high simmer and cook until peas are tender – roughly 5 minutes. Add remaining seasonings and continue to simmer until peas are tender and properly seasoned. If using, add ham in the last 5 to 10 minutes of cooking so it flavors but doesn't get over cooked. Taste and adjust seasonings to taste.

Pop's Pinto Beans

1-pound fresh pinto beans
4 cups water
1 medium onion, chopped
2 strips bacon, chopped into small pieces
ham hock or ham steak with bone (cut in pieces)
¾ teaspoon salt
½ teaspoon black pepper
1 teaspoon chili powder
1 teaspoon cumin
1 clove garlic, minced
1 tablespoon vegetable or canola oil

Put 1 tablespoon oil in Dutch oven or stock pot. Swirl to cover inside bottom of pot. Fry bacon until pliable but not completely cooked. Add chopped onion and cook over medium heat for about 5 minutes. Add minced garlic and cook 1 minute.

Add water to deglaze the pot. Add pintos and reduce heat to high simmer and cook until beans are almost tender. At this point, take a ½ cup of the pintos and mash with a fork. Return mashed pintos to pot to thicken the bean soup. Add remaining seasonings and continue to simmer until beans are tender and properly seasoned. If using, add ham in the last 5 to 10 minutes of cooking so it flavors but doesn't get over cooked. Taste beans and adjust seasoning as desired.

Refried Leftover Beans

Use leftover *Pop's Pinto Beans* to make refried beans. Use a 10" cast iron skillet, add beans to skillet to start heating. Mash and stir. Add a small amount of lard or bacon grease and continue to stir until beans are the proper refried consistency. Typically, Byron adds more grease, a little at a time, as he stirs to get the smoothness. Add salt and pepper to taste. Either serve from the skillet or put in a greased casserole dish and cover with shredded cheddar cheese and bake in an oven (preheated to 350 F) for 20 minutes or until the cheese is bubbly and beans are heated throughout.

Southern Fried Cabbage

3 slices of bacon
4 tablespoons of butter, divided
1 cup chopped onion
1 medium to large head of cabbage, chopped (10 cups)
1 teaspoon kosher or sea salt
¼ teaspoon of black pepper
1/4 teaspoon Cajun seasoning (optional)
2 teaspoons of apple cider vinegar
1/8 teaspoon dried red pepper flakes
1 oz. water

Chop the bacon and cook in the bottom of the pot until the fat is extracted. Add 2 tablespoons of the butter and onion and sauté for 4 minutes. Add a splash of water to the bottom of the pot to de-glaze and scrape the brown bits from the bottom of the pot. Add half the cabbage, salt, pepper and Cajun seasoning, stirring to combine. Add the remaining cabbage, stir, and reduce heat to a low simmer, covering pot and allow to cook for about 30 minutes or until the cabbage is tender.

Stir in the remaining 2 tablespoons of butter and cider vinegar; continue cooking until cabbage begins to brown around the edges. Taste and adjust seasonings as necessary.

Squash Casserole

12 cups (approximately 4 pounds) sliced yellow squash
1 cup chopped sweet onion
2/3 cup unsalted butter, divided
1 ½ tablespoons sugar
1 teaspoon salt
½ teaspoon black pepper
2 eggs, lightly beaten
1 sleeve of buttery crackers, crushed

Preheat oven to 350 degrees. In a Dutch oven over high heat, boil squash in enough water to cover until fork-tender or about 10 minutes. Remove from heat; drain well and return squash to Dutch oven off the stovetop.

In a small skillet over medium heat, sauté the onion in 1/3 cup butter until tender. Pour over squash. Add sugar, salt, pepper and egg to squash and stir gently to combine.

Pour mixture into a lightly greased 13 x 9" baking dish. Top with crushed crackers. Melt remaining 1/3 cup butter in a small skillet over low heat. Drizzle evenly over crushed crackers. Bake for 1 hour or until golden brown.

Cornbread Dressing

Hands down, my mother-in-law makes the best dressing I've ever tasted. Standing next to her, preparing dressing or other recipes together has been one of the highlights of my life. Even when I make the dressing now, I like to have her sitting in the kitchen with me.

1 pan of cornbread
6 slices white bread, cut in tiny cubes
3 large eggs
2 to 2 ½ cups low sodium chicken stock & turkey drippings
½ teaspoon pepper
1 teaspoon salt
½ cup chopped onion
½ cup chopped celery
¼ cup melted butter
1 ½ teaspoons dried sage
1 teaspoon poultry seasoning
½ teaspoon salt
½ teaspoon black pepper
½ cup milk or half and half

The night before serving, crumble cornbread and add to a large mixing bowl. Add the white bread cubes and seasonings. Cover with foil and set on counter for flavors to blend.

Preheat oven to 350 degrees. Heat 1/4 cup of butter in large pan over medium heat. Add celery and onion and cook until soft. Remove from heat and set aside to cool slightly. Add the onions and celery to the cornbread mixture and toss to combine.

In a mixing bowl, whisk together the milk and eggs and add to the bowl of cornbread mixture. Stir in two cups of chicken and/or turkey stock. The mixture will be very moist. Add more broth as necessary. Transfer the dressing to a greased 13 x 9" baking dish. Cut 2 tablespoons of butter into thin slices and scatter on top of dressing. Bake for 30 minutes or until light brown on top. Serve with Gravy.

Gravy for Dressing

Giblets, neck, organ meat
Water, to cover organ meat only
3 eggs, boiled and chopped into small pieces
1 ½ to 2 cups broth and/or turkey pan drippings
2 tablespoons flour or cornstarch
2 tablespoons butter
Salt and pepper, to taste

Boil organ meat and reserve liquid to thin gravy as needed. Once the meat is done, remove from liquid and allow to cool slightly. Cut up meat into very small pieces and set aside. In the same pan, mix the flour and the same measure of butter to form a roux. Cook for a few minutes until lightly golden.

To the roux, add the broth and mix well to avoid any lumps. Return the meat to the gravy and add the chopped eggs. Serve alongside cornbread dressing.

Roasted Harvest Vegetables

2 large sweet potatoes, scrubbed and cut into chunks
1 cup rutabaga, washed, peeled and cubed
2 small butternut squash, washed, peeled and cubed
2 cups
2 large carrots or 3 small carrots
3 to 4 sprigs Rosemary
¼ cup olive oil
½ teaspoon sea salt
¼ teaspoon black pepper

Preheat oven to 400 degrees. Mix the oil, rosemary, salt and pepper.

Toss vegetables in oil mixture and separate on a parchment-lined baking sheet. Roast for 40-50 minutes or until vegetables start to brown and are cooked through

Tomato Tart

My kids loved having this tart on Saturday nights when we watched movies together. Our family never argued about what to eat on movie night. However, there were some heated discussions about the movie selections!

2 tablespoons butter
1 large onion, thinly sliced in rings
Salt and pepper
1 pie dough for 9" pie *
¾ cup mozzarella cheese, shredded or sliced thin
1/8 cup fresh shredded parmesan cheese
1/8 cup Gruyere cheese, grated
1 ½ cups cherry tomatoes
Sprinkle of Italian seasoning (less than 1/8 teaspoon)
8 fresh basil leaves, sliced in thin strips or chiffonade

*Although homemade pie crust can't be beat, this pie works well with commercially prepared refrigerated pie dough.

Preheat oven to 450 degrees. Heat butter in a skillet over medium heat and add onions, salt and pepper. Cook onions until golden or about 5 to 7 minutes. Set aside to cool slightly.

On a lightly floured surface, roll pie dough to 1/8" thickness. Lay pie dough on a parchment covered baking sheet and crimp edges of dough to form a ridge around the dough. Sprinkle cheeses in bottom of pie dough, arrange caramelized onions over cheese. Arrange the tomatoes on top of cheese and onions. Sprinkle with Italian seasoning.

Bake tart for 15-18 minutes. If some of the tomatoes didn't "burst" while baking, carefully use the back of a wooden spoon to burst them. Allow the tart to sit for 5 minutes to absorb the juice of the tomatoes. Sprinkle the top of the tart with fresh basil and serve in large squares.

Texas Tomato Pie

9" pie dough
3 medium tomatoes, sliced (about 18 slices)
Salt to taste
Pinch of sugar
3 slices of bacon, cooked and crumbled, divided
1 small sweet onion (Vidalia), quartered and sliced thin (should measure about 1 cup)
3 cups shredded mozzarella, divided
¼ teaspoon black pepper
1/8 teaspoon garlic powder
2 tablespoons chopped fresh basil
1 cup mayonnaise *(do not use fat free or low fat)*
½ teaspoon hot sauce
1/8 cup of chopped parsley

Preheat oven to 400 degrees. Place the uncooked pie crust in a glass, deep dish pie pan and crimp the edges of the dough. Bake for 15 minutes or until the crust is just beginning to brown. Set aside to cool.

Line a baking sheet with two layers of paper towels. Slice the tomatoes about ¼" thickness and lay them out on the paper towels to drain. Sprinkle lightly with salt and cover with another layer of paper towels. Let tomatoes rest for 30 minutes while you prepare the bacon and onions. Cook the bacon until its crisp, remove set aside and sauté the onions in the bacon drippings until tender.

Reduce the oven temperature to 350 degrees. Add half a cup of the mozzarella cheese to the bottom of the cooled pie crust. Pat tomatoes to absorb as much moisture as possible. Remove any excess seeds of tomato slices and top cheese with a layer of tomatoes. Season with a sprinkle of black pepper and garlic powder. Add half of the basil, top with half of the onions and half of the bacon. Sprinkle a half cup of the cheese on top. Repeat layers, except the last layer of cheese, save that for topping.

In a mixing bowl, combine the mayonnaise, hot sauce, parsley and remaining 2 cups of cheese; spread evenly over the top. Bake at 350 degrees for about 40 to 45 minutes, or until bubbly and light golden brown on top. Shield edges of pie crust so it won't get too dark. Let pie cool to room temperature before slicing, using a serrated knife. Best served warm but also good cold. Store leftovers, if there are any, in the refrigerator.

Fried Green Tomatoes

2 cups all-purpose flour
3 whole green tomatoes
2 cups apple juice
5 eggs
1 dash hot sauce
2 cups cornmeal (seasoned with salt and pepper)
2 tablespoons fresh chopped basil
Small amount of oil for frying

Cut the tomatoes into 12 to 15 slices. Coat slices in flour. Dip in mixture of apple juice, eggs and hot sauce. Dip into mixture of cornmeal and basil. Fry in oil over medium heat until brown on both sides. Best served hot!

Nanny's Hominy Casserole

3 cans of hominy (drained and rinsed) (2 yellow, 1 white)
4 oz. can of chopped green chilies, drained
8 oz. container of sour cream or same amount of Greek yogurt
2 cups of white cheddar cheese, divided

Preheat oven to 350 degrees. Mix everything together except for 1 cup of cheese. Put in a greased 2-quart casserole dish. Sprinkle the remaining cheese evenly over the top of the casserole. Bake at 350 for 25 minutes or until bubbly. This always smells amazing and tastes even better. Thanks Nanny!

Byron's Collard Greens

Although I've made greens several times through the years, my husband makes the best collard greens you've ever tasted!

1 tablespoon olive oil
3 slices bacon
1 large onion, chopped
2 cloves garlic, minced
1 teaspoon salt
1 teaspoon pepper
3 cups chicken broth (low sodium)
1 pinch red pepper flakes
1-pound collard greens, washed, drained and cut in 2" pieces

Warm the oil in a large pot over medium heat. Add bacon, cooking until just crisp. Remove bacon to a plate lined with paper towels to drain, pat tops to remove any excess grease. Crumble the bacon and return to the pan. Add the onion and cook until tender. About 5 minutes.

Add garlic, cook until fragrant. Add collard greens and fry until they start to wilt. Pour in chicken broth, season with salt, pepper and red pepper flakes. Reduce heat to low, cover and simmer for 45 minutes or until tender. Serve hot with cornbread muffins.

Refried Beans

30 oz. refried beans
¼ cup Greek yogurt or sour cream
¼ cup chunky salsa
½ cup cheddar cheese

Preheat oven to 350 degrees. Spray an 8" x 8" baking pan with non-stick cooking spray. In a mixing bowl, combine beans, yogurt or sour cream, and salsa.

Pour bean mixture into the prepared baking dish and sprinkle cheese on top. Bake 20 minutes or until cheese is melted and bubbly.

Mexican Rice

1 cup uncooked long grain rice
2 cups low sodium chicken stock
1 tablespoon butter
½ cup chunky mild salsa
¾ teaspoon garlic salt
½ teaspoon ground cumin

Combine all ingredients into a large non-stick skillet. Bring to a boil, then cover and reduce heat to low. Simmer for 25 minutes. Remove from heat and let stand for 10 minutes before fluffing the rice with a fork.

Baked Beans

6 slices of bacon, cooked/chopped
4 regular size cans pork and beans
1 onion, chopped
½ cup Molasses
2 tablespoons mustard
¼ cup brown sugar
2 tablespoons butter

Preheat the oven to 350 degrees. Fry the bacon in a large skillet over medium high heat until crisp.

Remove the bacon from the pan, leaving the drippings and drain bacon on a paper towel. Crumble and set aside. Pour out and discard all but 2 tablespoons bacon drippings. Add 2 tablespoons butter. Add the onion and sauté until softened or about 7 minutes. Stir in beans and molasses, sugar, mustard and bacon. Mix well. Pour the beans into a 3-quart casserole dish and bake uncovered for 45 minutes.

Roasted Brussel Sprouts

This recipe is based on one given to me by my friend, Catherine. I revised the measurements slightly, doubled the sprouts and replaced the dried cranberries with dried cherries but the taste sensation was her invention. She is a fantastic cook and is quick to share recipes. Her dishes are always the first consumed at any of our potlucks.

2 lbs. Brussel Sprouts, washed, drained and halved
3 tablespoons olive oil
1 ½ tablespoons maple syrup
¼ to 1/3 cup dried cherries, rough chopped or left whole
1/3 cup chopped pecans
½ small tub blue cheese crumbles (also good with goat cheese but use less, probably ¼ cup)

Preheat oven to 350 degrees. Line a baking sheet with parchment paper and set aside. Combine olive oil and maple syrup in a gallon size Ziploc bag. Add Brussel Sprouts and toss to coat in the maple mixture. Put Brussel Sprouts on lined baking sheet and roast until browned and cooked through, about 20 minutes.

Immediately toss with cherries, pecans and blue cheese. The hot sprouts will melt some of the cheese and make a delicious sauce. Salt and pepper, to taste. Serve warm with ham, pork chops or roasted chicken.

My personal favorite way to enjoy this dish is to cook a ham steak, cut into bite-size pieces and add to the sprouts. It makes a wonderful one-dish meal.

Southern Sweet Potato Casserole

3 cups mashed cooked sweet potatoes
Butter to rub on outside of potatoes
½ cup sugar or to taste (up to 1 cup)
2 eggs, lightly beaten
1 teaspoon vanilla extract
1/3 cup whole milk or half and half
½ cup melted butter

Preheat oven to 425 degrees. Wash sweet potatoes and dry off, skins on. Using a fork, pierce several places on each potato. Rub outside of potato with butter and place on a parchment lined baking sheet. Bake for 30 minutes or until potatoes are fork tender. Peel and mash the sweet potatoes to equal 3 cups of mashed potatoes.

Reduce oven heat to 350 degrees. In a large mixing bowl, combine potatoes, sugar, eggs, vanilla, milk, and butter. Pour into a greased 2-quart casserole dish.

Topping

1 cup packed brown sugar
1/3 cup flour
¼ cup melted butter
1 cup chopped pecans

Stir together the topping ingredients and sprinkle on top of the sweet potato casserole. Bake for 30 minutes at 350 degrees.

Baked Mashed Potatoes

5 pounds potatoes
¾ cup butter (1 ½ sticks)
8 oz. cream cheese
½ cup half and half
¾ teaspoon salt
½ teaspoon black pepper

Preheat oven to 350 degrees. Wash, peel and cut potatoes into uniform chunks. In a large saucepan or Dutch oven, add potatoes and enough water to cover. Boil the potatoes until tender (approximate 20-30 minutes). Drain potatoes in a strainer. Return potatoes to the pot and mash.

Add 1 stick of butter, cream cheese and half and half. Add salt and pepper, to taste. Put mashed potatoes into a greased 13 x 9" baking dish and spread evenly. Top with pats of remaining butter (1/4 cup).

Place dish in pre-heated oven for 20-30 minutes. Serve hot.

World's Best Brownies

Chapter Seven
Perfect Endings

 In the south, dessert is one of the most important parts of a meal. Growing up in Texas, I seldom sat down to dinner that there wasn't something luscious waiting, if I ate all my vegetables. My mother, mother-in-law, and grandmothers were amazing cooks and could put together some of the best cakes, pies, and desserts. Many of the recipes you are about to read came from those ladies. Mamaw's cobbler was probably one of the best I've ever had. My grandfather always said it was the Best Dang Cobbler, hence the name. She used fresh fruit, cut in uniform slices and partnered with sugar and lemon juice in a saucepan where she would boil it for a few minutes to "marry" the flavors. This cobbler has a crust that raises around the cooked fruit and tastes buttery and light. My other grandmother, Ninnie, would use her buttermilk pie crust over cooked fruit to make a cobbler, dotting the top of the crust with little pats of butter. The crust on hers would end up making little wells of butter and you would hope for a piece that had the well. Both of these ladies' cobblers had rave reviews from anyone eating them.

 While Texans love their cobbler, pie is king. Staples include pecan, chocolate cream, coconut cream, or buttermilk. Buttermilk pie sounds like it would be overly tart and taste like buttermilk. Nothing could be further from the truth. A good buttermilk pie has a custard that is creamy and the top of the pie is almost candied in taste and appearance. Barb's chocolate pie is a recipe from my mother, Barbara, and is one of the better chocolate pies I've tasted. There were three kids in our immediate family, a sister six and a half years younger than me and an older brother who was six and a half years older than me. When my mother would make her chocolate pie, she always made two of them. One for my brother and one for the rest of the family. Her chocolate pie was not overly sweet but had excellent chocolate taste and if we didn't watch ourselves, we'd keep going back to the kitchen to cut another little sliver until we'd consumed way too much. Probably the most interestingly named pie is the Sawdust pie (not sure who came up with the name or why, but really?!). The sawdust pie reminds you of the frosting from a German chocolate cake. Coconut, graham crackers, pecans with plenty of sugar to make it syrupy good. The first time I had Sawdust Pie was in Comfort, Texas at a little pie shop. It didn't sound appetizing but looked different and smelled good so I gave it a try. I was so glad that I did! IT TASTES AMAZING. One thing I will tell you is that using graham crackers that you crush yourself instead of the graham cracker crumbs you buy at the grocery store makes a significant difference in flavor and moisture. Take the time to smash those graham crackers, you'll be glad you did.

You will also find a recipe for Mom's chocolate pudding that you really must try. When I was young, as with most girls my age, life could sometimes be devastating and there was a need for comfort. When I had an issue, challenge or just a bad day, my mother would tell me to change into my play clothes and meet her at the kitchen table. I would go to my room, change into jeans and a tee shirt and sneakers and return to the kitchen. By the time I was halfway down the hall, I could smell chocolate and butter. My mood would automatically and immediately improve and I would pick up the pace to make it to the kitchen. Instead of meeting her at the kitchen table, I would sit on the stool next to the stovetop while she stirred the chocolate pudding until it was smooth and thick. She would have me continue to stir while she located small custard cups and buttered them. She poured chocolate happiness into those cups and set them on the counter to cool. She would put one on the kitchen table for me to consume immediately and the others she would cool slightly and move to the refrigerator for that evening's dessert. There was little during those formative years that couldn't be resolved or made better by Mom's chocolate pudding.

Peach Cobbler Snack Cake

1 cup sugar plus 3 teaspoons, divided
2 ½ cups sliced peaches
½ teaspoon corn starch
2 cups all-purpose flour
½ teaspoon salt
2 ½ teaspoons baking powder
1 ½ cups whole milk
3 tablespoons unsalted butter, melted and cooled

Preheat oven to 350 degrees. Spray an 8" x 8" baking pan with non-stick cooking spray and set aside.

In a small bowl, combine 3 tablespoons sugar and corn starch. Toss peaches in the mixture and coat evenly. Set aside.

In a medium bowl, stir together 1 cup sugar, flour, salt and baking powder. In another bowl, whisk together milk and butter. Slowly pour wet ingredients into dry ingredients, add peaches and stir until combined.

Pour cake batter into prepared baking dish. Bake in preheated oven for 1 hour or until center, when tested with a wooden pick, comes out clean.

My husband takes this snack cake to work to share for breakfast. It is also good for a lighter dessert when topped with a little whipped cream. (or a lot...your choice)

This cake will remain fresh for up to three days, ...*but it won't last that long!*

Mom's Coca Cola Cake

Cake:
½ cup coca cola (real coke)
¼ cup vegetable oil (I use Canola)
¼ cup unsalted butter
1 ½ tablespoons cocoa powder
1 cup sugar
1 cup all-purpose or cake flour
¼ teaspoon salt
½ teaspoon baking soda
1 egg room temperature (set out 30 minutes ahead or immerse in warm water for 5 minutes)
¼ cup buttermilk
¾ teaspoon vanilla

Preheat oven to 350 degrees. Spray an 8" x 8" baking pan with non-stick cooking spray, set aside. In a large bowl, whisk together sugar, flour, salt and baking soda, set aside. In saucepan over medium heat, whisk together the coca cola, oil butter and cocoa powder and whisk until smooth and bring to a boil, pour over flour/sugar mixture. Beat with hand mixer until combined. Add in eggs, buttermilk, and vanilla and beat again until smooth.

Pour into prepared pan and bake for 30-35 minutes until center is set. Remove from oven and poke holes all over the top of the cake with a fork.

Frosting:
¼ cup butter
1 tablespoon cocoa powder
4 tablespoons milk or half and half
½ teaspoon vanilla
2 cups powdered sugar

To make frosting in saucepan, melt together butter, cocoa powder and milk. Bring to a gentle boil, stirring frequently. Remove from heat and immediately whisk in powdered sugar and vanilla until smooth.

Pour over warm cake and gently press down into holes.

Let cool for about 30 minutes to give frosting time to set up. Great served with ice cream (but what isn't great with ice cream?)

Texas Tornado Cake

Cake
2 cups all-purpose or cake flour
2 teaspoons baking soda
2 cups sugar
2 large eggs, lightly beaten
½ teaspoon vanilla extract
20 oz. crushed pineapple, undrained

Preheat oven to 350 degrees. Mix all cake ingredients with a wooden spoon. Pour into greased 13 x 9" baking pan and bake for 30-40 minutes or until center of the cake is done.

Frosting
½ cup butter (1 stick)
¾ cup evaporated milk
1 cup sugar
1 cup chopped pecans
1 cup shredded coconut

Cook butter, evaporated milk and sugar in a medium saucepan over medium heat for about 5 minutes, stirring often. Add nuts and coconut. Frost cake after both the cake and frosting have cooled somewhat.

This is a family favorite and so easy to put together in less than an hour.

Apple Spice Cake

1 ½ cups all-purpose or cake flour
1 cup of sugar
½ teaspoon baking soda
½ teaspoon salt
½ teaspoon cinnamon
2 large eggs, lightly beaten
½ cup canola oil
1 teaspoon vanilla extract
1 ½ cups finely chopped apples
½ cup chopped pecans

Preheat the oven to 350 degrees. Grease an 8" x 8" baking pan and set aside. In a medium bowl, combine flour, sugar, baking soda, salt, & cinnamon. Stir with a whisk to mix thoroughly.

In another bowl, mix the eggs with a hand mixer until light in color and foamy. Add the oil and vanilla and beat well.

Stir in the flour mixture with a spoon and continue stirring until the flour disappears into the batter. Add apples and nuts and stir to mix them. Spoon batter into the prepared pan and bake for 40 to 45 minutes, or until a wooden pick inserted in the center comes out clean. Place the hot cake on a wire rack and prepare the glaze.

Brown Sugar Glaze

½ cup packed light brown sugar
2 tablespoons butter
½ teaspoon vanilla extract

Combine all ingredients for the glaze into a small saucepan. Cook over medium heat, stirring often, until mixture comes to a boil. Cook for 3 to 5 minutes.

Spoon the hot glaze over the still hot from the oven cake. Let the glazed cake cool completely before serving.

Gingerbread Pound Cake with Lemon Sauce

1 cup unsalted butter
1 cup sugar
5 large eggs, room temperature and lightly beaten
2 cups all-purpose flour
½ teaspoon baking soda
¾ teaspoon ground ginger
1 teaspoon ground cinnamon
1/2 teaspoon ground cloves
1 cup molasses
½ cup sour cream
Sifted confectioner's sugar

Preheat oven to 325 degrees. Spray a 10" Bundt or tube pan with non-stick cooking spray and set aside.

Cream butter and sugar, beating at medium speed in a stand mixer. Add eggs, one at a time, beating well after each addition. Combine flour, soda and spices. Set aside. Combine molasses and sour cream. Add flour mixture alternately with molasses, beginning and ending with flour mixture. Mix just until combined.

Pour batter into prepared pan and bake for 1 hour. Cool at least 15 minutes before removing from pan. When cake is cooled, sprinkle with confectioner's sugar and serve with lemon sauce.

Lemon Sauce

½ cup sugar
2 tablespoons cornstarch
1 cup water1 tablespoons butter
2 teaspoons lemon zest
1/3 cup fresh lemon juice

For sauce, cook first 3 ingredients over medium heat stirring with a wire whisk. When thick and smooth, remove from heat and add lemon juice, zest and butter. Pour into a syrup pitcher or gravy boat to serve with gingerbread pound cake or your favorite gingerbread.

Pineapple Upside Down Cake

Topping

5 tablespoons unsalted butter, melted
½ cup packed light brown sugar
6 to 8 slices of pineapple (fresh or canned, save juice)
15 maraschino cherries, stems removed

Preheat oven to 350 degrees. Spray a 10" skillet with non-stick cooking spray. Then, pour melted butter into the bottom of the skillet and sprinkle ½ cup packed brown sugar evenly over the top. Arrange the pineapple slices and cherries on top of the butter mixture. Set aside

Cake

1 1/3 cups all-purpose or cake flour
2 teaspoons baking powder
½ teaspoon salt
¾ cup packed light brown sugar
¼ cup unsalted butter
¾ cup whole milk
1 teaspoon vanilla extract
1 large egg, room temperature and lightly beaten
3 tablespoons pineapple juice

In a medium bowl, whisk together flour, baking powder and salt. Set aside. In a large bowl, beat the remaining brown sugar and butter together until smooth. Turn the mixer to low and slowly add the milk, vanilla, egg and pineapple juice until combined. Add dry ingredients to the wet mixture beating only until combined.

Pour the batter over the pineapple slices and spread evenly. Bake for 45 minutes or until golden brown and the top springs back when pressed with your finger. Allow the cake to cool in the pan for 5 minutes and then turn the cake out onto a cake plate r patter and leave the pan on the cake for 10 minutes longer. Remove the pan and allow to cool to room temperature or serve warm, if desired.

Sugar Cream Pie

Pie
4 tablespoons cornstarch
¾ cup sugar
4 tablespoons butter, melted and cooled to room temperature
2 ¼ cups heavy cream
1 tablespoon vanilla extract
Pie Crust Dough for 9" pie

Topping
4 tablespoons butter, melted
¼ cup cinnamon sugar (1/4 cup sugar + 2 teaspoons cinnamon)

Preheat oven to 325 degrees. Form the pie crust dough in a 9" pie pan and flute edges. Set the pie plate in the center of a parchment lined baking sheet. Bake pie crust for 10 minutes and remove from oven to cool.

In a small bowl, mix the cornstarch and sugar until blended. In a medium saucepan, bring the cornstarch-sugar mixture, melted butter, and heavy cream together over medium heat, stirring constantly. The mixture is done when it's thick and creamy. Remove from heat and stir in vanilla.

Pour mixture into the prepared pie crust and smooth out the top, drizzle on the melted butter and evenly sprinkle on the cinnamon sugar. Bake for 25 minutes, then turn on the broiler and broil for about 1 minute, watching carefully, remove from oven and allow to come to room temperature before refrigerating for at least 1 hour to set. Store in refrigerator. **(This pie, like revenge, is best served cold!)**

Buttermilk Pie Crust preparation

Buttermilk Pie Crust

(food processor method - makes two 9" crusts - use one and freeze the other for up to a month. Thaw for 20 minutes then roll out crust.)

1 cup (2-sticks) unsalted butter, cold and cut in ½" chunks)
2 ½ cups all-purpose or pastry flour
1 tablespoon sugar
1 teaspoon salt
½ to 2/3 cup buttermilk

Before you measure out ingredients, cut butter into chunks and place in freezer. Stir together flour, sugar, and salt and put in the bowl of a food processor. Add butter and pulse until butter is cut into flour with "pea size" pieces of butter throughout. While pulsing, slowly pour in ½ cup buttermilk. At this point, the dough should look like rough crumbs, but should hold together if squeezed between your fingers. If needed, add more buttermilk one teaspoon at a time to gain the correct consistency.

Lay a sheet of parchment paper on the counter with a layer of plastic wrap on top of that. Dump half of the dough onto the sheet. Gather edges and press tightly to form a 1" thick disk. Repeat with the other half of the mixture. Refrigerate for at least one hour before rolling to fit your pie pan.

Buttermilk Pie

My daughter loves this buttermilk pie. She always told me Nanny's was better though! So, I asked Nanny about it. Our ingredients were essentially the same, but her baking procedure was different. Sure enough, I tried her method and it improved the consistency of the custard! Here's the mash up of our methods.

½ cup buttermilk
1 ¾ cups sugar
2 large eggs, lightly beaten
3 tablespoons all-purpose flour
½ cup (1 stick) unsalted butter melted and cooled
1 teaspoon vanilla
Pinch of salt
1 9" unbaked pie crust

Preheat oven to 400 degrees. In a large mixing bowl, combine buttermilk, sugar, eggs, flour, butter, vanilla, and salt until mixed and pour into the unbaked pie crust.

Bake 15 minutes. Reduce oven temperature to 350 degrees and bake another 30-45 minutes or until center is set. Once the crust is golden, tent the crust edges with foil to make sure it doesn't get too brown.

Sawdust Pie

1 ½ cups flaked coconut
1 ½ cups graham cracker crumbs
1 ½ chopped pecans
1 ½ cup sugar
1 cup egg whites (5 to 7 eggs depending on size)
Pie Dough for a 9" pie

　　Preheat oven to 450 degrees. Cover pie shell with two layers of foil and bake for 8 minutes. Remove foil and bake 4 minutes or until golden brown. Cool on a wire rack.

　　Reduce oven temperature to 350 degrees. Combine coconut, graham cracker crumbs, pecans and sugar in a large bowl. In another bowl, beat egg white just until foamy; add to the coconut mixture. Mix well. Pour into prepared pie shell. Bake uncovered for 30 minutes or until set.

　　Serve with a scoop of vanilla ice cream or a dollop of whipped cream.

Sweet Potato Pecan Pie

2 pounds sweet potatoes, about 5 medium size sweet potatoes
2 tablespoons unsalted butter, softened
2 egg yolks
1 whole egg
1/3 cup sugar
¼ cup maple syrup
½ teaspoon salt
1/3 teaspoon allspice
½ teaspoon cinnamon
1 teaspoon vanilla extract
½ cup buttermilk
Praline Topping
3 tablespoons unsalted butter
3 tablespoons packed light brown sugar
3 tablespoons pure maple syrup
1 ½ tablespoons milk
¾ cup chopped pecans

    Prepare the pastry and line a 9" pie pan. Trim the dough and flute the edges. Place the pie shell in the refrigerator for an hour to prevent shrinkage. Preheat oven to 425 degrees. Line the chilled pastry with two sheets of heavy foil, then fill with 2 cups dried beans or pie weights. Bake for 20 minutes. Remove foil and weights and bake crust until light golden or about 10 minutes longer.

    Reduce oven temperature to 350 degrees. Wash sweet potatoes and prick with a fork, place on parchment lined baking sheet and bake for 20-30 minutes, depending on the size of the potatoes. Cool them for at least 10 minutes, then cut in half and scoop out potato with a spoon into a medium mixing bowl. Discard potato skins. There should be 2 cups of potato. Add 2 tablespoons butter and mash potatoes with a potato masher or fork.

    In a medium mixing bowl, whisk together egg yolks, egg, sugar, maple syrup, salt, allspice, cinnamon, vanilla and buttermilk. Add the egg mixture to the sweet potatoes and fold together gently until combined.

Place pie pan on a lined baking sheet. Pour the sweet potato filling into the pie crust. Use little strips of foil to create a collar and shield the edges of the crust to prevent over-browning. Bake for a total of 40 minutes. After the pie has been in the oven for 30 minutes, make the praline topping.

In a small saucepan melt the butter over medium heat. Stir in the brown sugar, maple syrup, and milk. Cook, stirring constantly, until the mixture comes to a boil. While the pie is in the oven remove foil from around the edge of the crust. Sprinkle the pecans over the partially baked pie then carefully pour the hot brown sugar mixture over the pecans. Bake for another 15 minutes or until the center of the pie appears set.

Cool pie for at least 1 hour. Cover and refrigerate until ready to serve.

Pecan Pie

1 cup light corn syrup
¾ cup sugar
¼ cup light brown sugar
2 tablespoons unsalted butter, melted and cooled
2 teaspoons vanilla
½ teaspoon salt
3 eggs, room temperature then lightly beaten
1 ¼ cups roughly chopped pecans
Pecan halves for decorating top of pie (about ½ cup)
1 9" pie crust dough

    Preheat oven to 350 degrees. In a large mixing bowl, beat together eggs, vanilla, syrup, and melted butter. Stir in chopped pecans and mix well. Pour mixture into a 9" unbaked pie crust and place pecan halves decoratively on top. Bake for 45 to 50 minutes or until center is set.

Coconut Cream Pie

Filling
¾ cup sugar
1/3 cup cornstarch
3 cups half and half
2 egg yolks
1 large egg
1 cup sweetened shredded coconut
1 teaspoon vanilla extract
9" pie crust dough

Preheat oven to 400 degrees. Roll and form pie crust into a 9" pie pan and bake for 10 minutes or until crust is a golden hue. **Allow crust to cool completely before adding filling.**

Spread ¼ cup coconut (topping ingredients) on a parchment lined baking sheet. Bake until toasted and starting to brown. Set aside to top the pie later.

Combine the sugar, cornstarch, egg, egg yolks and half and half in a medium saucepan and whisk together until it comes to a boil. Boil for 1 to 2 minutes and remove from heat. Stir in coconut and vanilla. Pour into pie crust and chill until firm.

Topping
2 cups heavy cream
½ cup sugar
½ teaspoon vanilla extract
½ teaspoon coconut extract
¼ cup toasted coconut

Whip heavy cream at high speed. Slowly add ½ cup sugar, vanilla and coconut extract. Beat until stiff peaks form. Spread whipped cream over pie and sprinkle with toasted coconut. Refrigerate until ready to serve.

Barb's Chocolate Pie

1 ¼ cups sugar
½ cup all-purpose flour
¼ cup cocoa
Dash of salt
4 egg yolks
2 cups whole milk
¼ cup butter
1 teaspoon vanilla extract
9" pie crust dough

    Preheat oven to 350 F. Bake pie crust until golden – approximately 10-15 minutes. In a large saucepan, combine sugar, flour, cocoa and a dash of salt. In a mixing bowl, combine milk and egg yolks. Stir milk and egg yolks into mixture, add butter. Cook over medium heat and stir constantly until filling thickens and starts a low boil. Remove from heat; stir in vanilla, spoon into pastry shell.

    You can put a meringue on top if you want, using the egg whites remaining from 4 eggs, 1/8 teaspoon cream of tartar, and 1 tablespoon sugar. Whip until soft peaks form, mound egg white mixture on top of pie, spreading to edges and bake in the oven just until top starts to lightly brown, about 5-8 minutes.

Hello Dolly Squares

1 ½ cups graham cracker crumbs
½ cup (1 stick) butter
¼ cup sugar
2 cups chocolate chips
1 cup chopped walnuts
1 cup coconut
1 can sweetened condensed milk

Preheat oven to 350 degrees. Spray or butter an 8" x 8" pan and set aside. Melt butter and add graham cracker crumbs and sugar. Mix then pat into either an 8"x8 square pan.

Sprinkle pecans or walnuts over the crust, then chocolate chips and finish layers with coconut. Drizzle the sweetened condensed milk evenly over cookie bars. Bake for 25 minutes. Cool and cut into small squares. Rich, gooey and delicious.

Chocolate dipped coconut macaroons

Chocolate Dipped Coconut Macaroons

At Christmas or another holiday or special occasion, my son Max almost always requested coconut macaroons. He was always the most polite and thoughtful child and one day when he was very young he walked up and told me he had done well in his talented and gifted program. I told him I was so proud of him and what could I do to help him celebrate. He looked up at me with big brown eyes and said, "well, if it isn't too much trouble, could you make some of those cookies that are stacked up?" After several questions, I realized he wanted coconut macaroons. I leave mine as shaped by the cookie scoop, so they are "stacked up" mounds of coconut. Dipping these cookies in chocolate takes them to a higher plain.

14 ounces sweetened coconut flakes
¾ cup sweetened condensed milk
1 teaspoon vanilla extract
2 large egg whites
¼ teaspoon salt
4 ounces semi-sweet or dark chocolate bar

Preheat oven to 325 degrees and line a large baking sheet with parchment paper and set aside.

In a large bowl, stir together coconut flakes, condensed milk and vanilla extract until combined. In a separate bowl, combine the egg whites and salt. (make sure the bowl is clean and dry). Beat egg whites and salt until stiff peaks form.

Gently fold the egg whites into the coconut mixture until completely combined. Using a 1 ½ tablespoon-sized cookie scoop, scoop macaroon mixture into balls and drop onto prepared baking sheet, place at least an inch apart.

Bake for 20 to 25 minutes or until tops are just beginning to turn golden brown. Allow coconut macaroons to cool completely before dipping in chocolate. To dip in chocolate - chop the chocolate bar into small, even-sized pieces and place in a small microwave-safe bowl. Heat in the microwave in 20-second intervals, stirring between, until the chocolate is fully melted and smooth. Dip the bottom of each macaroon into chocolate and return to parchment covered baking sheet for the chocolate to harden. If you are in a hurry, you may set the baking sheet, with dipped cookies, in the refrigerator to harden the chocolate more quickly.

Bebe's Lemon Bars

Crust
½ cup unsalted butter, softened
1 1/3 cups all-purpose or pastry flour
¼ cup sugar

Pre-heat oven to 350 degrees. Grease an 8" x 8" (square) baking pan. In a mixing bowl, combine flour and sugar. Add the softened butter and mix until the butter is evenly distributed. Pat the crust evenly in the pan. Bake for 15 minutes or until edges start to lightly brown. Set aside to cool slightly.

Filling
2 large eggs, room temperature then lightly beaten
2 tablespoons all-purpose flour
¾ cup sugar
¼ teaspoon baking powder
4 tablespoons fresh lemon juice
3 tablespoons confectioner's sugar

In a separate mixing bowl, combine all filling ingredients except confectioner's sugar and pour over crust and return to oven and bake for 18 to 20 minutes. Cool bars prior to sprinkling with confectioner's sugar. Cut into small squares to serve.

Granny Mobley's Sugar Cookies

1 egg
1 cup sugar
¾ shortening (or 1/2 cup shortening and ¼ cup butter)
1 teaspoon vanilla
2 teaspoons baking powder
½ cup whole milk
Pinch of salt

Cream sugar and butter/shortening until fluffy. Add egg and mix again. Add part milk, some flour then remainder of milk, end with remaining flour. Sprinkle powdered sugar on a flat surface and roll the dough to ¼" thickness and cut with cookie cutters.

Sprinkle with sugar and bake for 10 minutes. Cool then frost.

I always organize my ingredients before I start

World's Best Brownies – frosting sandwiched between the layers

World's Best Brownies

(according to my son, Max)

½ cup cooking oil (or ¼ cup oil, ¼ cup butter)
1 cup sugar
4 eggs
1 teaspoon vanilla
16 oz. can chocolate syrup
1 ¼ cups flour, sift after measuring
¼ teaspoon baking soda
1 cup chopped pecans
Preheat oven to 350 degrees.

Choose your pan size: half sheet for thinner more cake-like brownies, or a quarter sheet for thicker chewy brownies.

In a large mixing bowl, blend sugar and cooking oil. Beat in eggs and vanilla. Blend in chocolate syrup, flour, and salt. Stir in nuts. Pour in greased cookie sheet and bake at 350 degrees for 30 to 35 minutes. Top with quick frosting.

For cake-like use a **half sheet pan**, reduce baking time by 5 minutes. I add frosting sandwiched between two layers of cake-like brownies for variety.

Quick Frosting:

(also great for white, yellow or chocolate cake)

½ cup (1 stick) butter
4 tablespoons cocoa
6 tablespoons milk or half and half
16 oz. (1 box) powdered sugar
1 tablespoon vanilla
1 cup chopped pecans

Mix cocoa and milk in a saucepan over medium heat. Melt and bring to a low boil (small bubbles). Remove from heat, stir in powdered sugar and vanilla. At this point, either add the chopped pecans to the frosting mixture, or hold off and sprinkle them after frosting the brownies.

Snickerdoodles

¾ cup sugar
½ cup unsalted butter, room temperature
1 large egg, room temperature then lightly beaten
½ teaspoon vanilla extract
1 ¾ cups all-purpose flour
½ teaspoon cream of tartar
¼ teaspoon baking soda
½ teaspoon baking powder
¼ teaspoon salt

Topping

1 tablespoon sugar
1 tablespoon cinnamon

Preheat oven to 350 degrees. Line a baking sheet with parchment paper and set aside. In the bowl of a stand mixer, cream together the butter and sugar. Add the egg and vanilla. In a separate bowl, stir together the flour, baking powder, baking soda, cream of tartar and salt. Slowly add the flour mixture to the egg/sugar mixture. Mix only until just combined. Chill dough for a minimum of 2 hours.

Remove dough from refrigerator and roll into balls of about 3 tablespoons or a large cookie scoop. Roll each cookie in the topping mixture and place at least 3 inches apart on the baking sheet. Bake cookies for 12 minutes or until the first brown starts to appear. Once baked, these cookies will last, in a sealed container, for up to 3 days. Recipe yields about 16 cookies.

Gingerbread Molasses Cookies

¾ cup all-purpose flour
1 teaspoon ground ginger
½ teaspoon baking soda
¼ teaspoon ground cinnamon
1/8 teaspoon ground cloves
1/8 teaspoon salt
4 tablespoons butter, softened
1/3 cup sugar
1 egg yolk
1 teaspoon water
2 tablespoons molasses
4 teaspoons sugar for tops of cookies

Preheat oven to 350 degrees. Line a baking sheet with parchment paper and set aside.

Mix the flour, ginger, baking soda, cinnamon, cloves and salt in a bowl and set aside. In the bowl of a stand mixer, cream the butter and 1/3 cup sugar until light and fluffy. Beat in the egg yolk and then mix in the water and molasses. Gradually add the flour mixture into the molasses mixture.

Spray a medium cookie scoop with non-stick cooking spray. Scoop out a walnut-size ball of dough. Drop the cookie ball in a shallow dish, containing the 4 teaspoons of sugar, and roll to coat. Place the cookies 2 inches apart but do not flatten them. Bake for 10 minutes.

Allow the cookies to cool on the baking sheet for 5 minutes then transfer them to a wire rack to cool completely. This recipe makes approximately 12 cookies which can be stored in an airtight container for several days, if they last that long.

Texas Cow Chips

2 cups butter
2 cups each of white and brown sugar
4 eggs, lightly beaten
2 tablespoons vanilla extract
4 cups flour
½ teaspoon salt
2 teaspoons each of baking powder and baking soda
2 cups each of oatmeal and bran flake cereals
1 cup chopped pecans
1 cup shredded coconut
1 cup raisins
12 oz. bag of chocolate chips
6 oz. bag of peanut butter chips

Preheat oven to 350 degrees. Line a baking sheet with parchment paper and set aside. In a bowl of a stand mixer, beat butter and sugars together until well blended. Add eggs and vanilla and beat until smooth. In a separate bowl, combine flour, salt, baking powder and soda; gradually add to sugar mixture and stir well. Stir in remaining ingredients.

Refrigerate cookie dough for about an hour. Using a ¼ measuring cup or large cookie scoop, drop cookies onto the prepared baking sheet. Limit 6 per baking sheet as the cookies will spread. Bake for 12 to 15 minutes. Cool on a wire rack and store between sheets of parchment in an airtight container.

Cranberry White Chocolate Oatmeal Cookies

1 ½ cups old fashioned oats
1 cup all-purpose flour
¾ teaspoon baking powder
½ teaspoon baking soda
½ teaspoon ground cinnamon
1/8 teaspoon ground cloves
½ teaspoon salt
½ cup unsalted butter, melted
½ teaspoon vanilla extract
½ cup packed light brown sugar
¼ cup sugar
1 large egg, lightly beaten
¾ cup dried cranberries or dried cherries
1 cup white chocolate chips

In a large mixing bowl, whisk together all dry ingredients. In a separate bowl, mix butter, vanilla, and egg. Stir this mixture into the dry ingredients. Add white chocolate chips and dried cranberries or cherries. Cover bowl and *refrigerate at least 2 hours or overnight*.

Preheat oven to 350 degrees. Line a baking sheet with parchment paper. Scoop dough with a medium sized cookie scoop, spacing 2 inches apart. Bake cookies 13-15 minutes. Cool, then transfer to an airtight container or cookie jar.

These are especially popular during the holidays.

Pecan Tassies

Tart Dough
3 cups all-purpose or pastry flour
¼ cup sugar
Pinch of salt
8 ounces butter, *cut into small pieces and freeze before starting*
2 large eggs, lightly beaten
2 to 4 tablespoons water (add 1 tablespoon at a time until proper consistency)

In the bowl of a food processor, combine flour, sugar and salt and pulse until mixed. Add eggs and water until dough forms. Remove from food processor and knead a few minutes. Form dough into 2 balls and flatten each into a thick disc and chill for at least 30 minutes.

On a floured surface, roll out dough into a thin (1/8") sheet. Using a 1 ½ to 2" biscuit cutter to cut as many circles as possible from the dough. Roll together any scraps to make additional circles.

Grease a mini-muffin pan with non-stick cooking spray and fit a circle into each muffin mold. Prick bottom with fork and form up sides to appear like a tiny pie. Put the muffin pan in the refrigerator until filling is finished and the Tassies are ready to bake.

Filling
¾ cup white sugar
¼ cup light brown sugar (firmly packed)
1 cup corn syrup (I use light, but light or dark will work)
¾ teaspoon vanilla extract
1/3 cup melted unsalted butter
3 eggs, lightly beaten
1 cup finely chopped pecan pieces

Preheat oven to 350 degrees. Sprinkle a small number of pecans in the bottom of each tart shell in the mini muffin tin.

Combine sugar, brown sugar, corn syrup, vanilla, butter and eggs. Stir to combine. Carefully pour syrup over the pecans in each tart shell to within 1/8" of top. Keep filling inside the pastry. Bake 20 to 25 minutes or until lightly golden. Remove the muffin tin from the oven and allow to cool for a few minutes before removing from the tin and placing cookies on a cooling rack (about 10 minutes). Store in an airtight container once cooled completely.

Ali's Peanut Butter Cookies

When my granddaughter was about five years old, she wants to make cookies, "all by myself Grammy". I found this simple cookie recipe and talked her through the measurements and helped with placement in the oven & later removal. She "nailed it!" We used brown sugar so the cookies were more chewy. Her sense of accomplishment was worth all the calories I consumed.

1 cup peanut butter
1 large egg, lightly beaten
1 cup sugar, firmly packed brown OR white sugar *
1 cup chocolate chips.

Preheat oven to 350 degrees. Line a baking sheet with parchment paper and set aside.

In a large mixing bowl, combine peanut butter, egg, sugar and chocolate chips, stirring with a wooden spoon. Form into balls and roll in sugar, if desired. Bake for 8 to 10 minutes.

*granulated sugar gives the cookie a sandy texture while brown sugar provides a chewier cookie. Firmly packed means press the moist brown sugar into the measuring cup.

Pecan Puffs

½ cup butter or margarine (1 stick)
2 Tablespoons. sugar
1 teaspoon vanilla
1 cup chopped pecans
1 cup CAKE flour
Pinch of salt
1 lb. confectioner's sugar (powdered sugar)
Paper bag

Preheat oven to 300 degrees. Line a baking sheet with parchment paper and set aside.

In a large mixing bowl, cream butter and sugar until creamy. Add vanilla, flour and pecans, stirring just to combine. Refrigerate dough for at least 30 minutes and scoop dough to make 1" balls. Place on prepared baking sheet and bake for 20-25 minutes or until very lightly browned.

Remove from oven and allow to cool at least 5 minutes. Put confectioner's sugar in paper bag and gently drop in a few cookies at a time and carefully jiggle bag to cover each cookie completely in sugar. Store in an airtight container.

These buttery clouds of cookie melt in your mouth and if you aren't careful, you will eat a dozen without realizing it, they are so good.

Best Dang Blackberry Cobbler

½ cup unsalted butter (1 stick)
2 cups of sugar; divided (you will use one cup in the fruit mixture and one cup in the batter)
4 cups Blackberries –cut in half, take care not to use too much juice.
1 tablespoon lemon juice
1 cup all-purpose flour
1 tablespoon baking powder
¼ teaspoon salt
1 cup milk or half and half

Preheat oven to 375 degrees. Melt butter in a cast iron skillet. Remove from oven when melted. Bring mixture of fruit, one cup of sugar, and lemon juice to a boil in a medium saucepan. Remove from heat.

Mix flour, one cup sugar, baking powder, and salt in a medium mixing bowl. Add milk and mix until combined. Pour batter on top of melted butter, do not stir! Pour fruit over batter, again, do not stir. (the batter will rise around the fruit)

Bake for 35-45 minutes or until the top of the cobbler is golden. Serve with ice cream.

This basic batter is great for most cobblers. Here are some variations.

Peach cobbler: use **four cups of sliced peaches, 1 teaspoon cinnamon, 1 teaspoon vanilla, ¼ cup chopped pecans**. (no lemon zest or lemon juice)

Strawberry cobbler: use **four cups of sliced strawberries, zest from half of an orange, 1 tablespoon fresh orange juice** (no lemon zest/no lemon juice), **OR** use **1 teaspoon almond extract, ¼ cup sliced almonds** with the **strawberries** in place of the fruit zest and citrus juice.

Cherry Clafoutis

Cherry Clafoutis

1 lb. fresh sweet cherries, stemmed and pitted
2 tablespoons butter, melted
4 large eggs, room temperature then lightly beaten
1 cup milk or half-and-half
¾ cup all-purpose flour
¼ teaspoon salt
½ cup sugar
½ teaspoon almond extract
½ teaspoon vanilla extract
Powdered (Confectioner's) sugar for dusting after baking

   Preheat oven to 350 degrees. Butter a round 9" or 10" baking dish. Dust with 2 tablespoons sugar. Arrange the cherries in a single layer. Mix eggs with remaining sugar and salt. Stir in flour, add milk, vanilla, almond extract and mix well until well blended. Add melted butter and stir to combine. Pour the mixture over cherries and bake for 40 to 45 minutes. Cool until it deflates somewhat. Sprinkle cooled clafoutis with powdered sugar. Serve warm or chilled.

   This dish serves as a light custardy dessert after a big meal. In France, clafoutis is eaten at any time of the day and is especially enjoyed for breakfast. Although tasty warm, my preference is to chill overnight and have a cold version the next day.

Mom's Chocolate Pudding

(Yields 4-6 normal servings or 1 - 2 extra-large, bad day, comfort servings.)

1 cup granulated sugar
¼ corn starch
¼ cup plus 2 tablespoons unsweetened cocoa powder
1/8 teaspoon kosher salt
4 cups heavy cream
2 large egg yolks, lightly beaten
2 teaspoons vanilla extract

In a heavy medium saucepan, stir together sugar, cornstarch, cocoa powder, and salt. Gradually whisk in the cream and egg yolks.

Place over medium heat and cook; stirring frequently, until the mixture comes to a boil, about 20 minutes. Reduce heat to simmer, stirring constantly, for 1 minute longer, then remove from the heat and stir in vanilla extract.

Transfer the pudding to individual serving bowls or glasses, cover and refrigerate until well chilled.

Banana Pudding

4 bananas sliced
8 large eggs, separated
2 ½ cups sugar
¼ pound butter
6 cups whole milk
2 tablespoons vanilla extract
3 tablespoons cornstarch
1 large box vanilla wafers

Preheat oven to 350 degrees. Spray a 2-quart baking or casserole dish with non-stick cooking spray and set aside. In a large saucepan, combine the milk, egg yolks, sugar, cornstarch and butter. Cook over medium heat until mixture thickens. Add vanilla.

Layer vanilla wafers in the bottom of the baking dish, follow with a layer of sliced bananas and a small amount of pudding. Repeat layers until all cookies and bananas have been used. Pour remaining pudding over the top of the dish.

In the bowl of a standing mixer, beat egg whites with 8 tablespoons of sugar until soft peaks form. Cover the pudding with meringue and bake 15 minutes. Serve warm out of the oven or refrigerate and serve chilled.

Super Easy Vanilla Ice Cream I

2 cups half and half
1 cup heavy cream
1 ½ teaspoons vanilla extract
½ cup sugar

Combine all ingredients in a mixing bowl, mix well. If using an electric ice cream machine, pour mixture through the hole in the lid and churn for 20-40 minutes or until desired consistency.

To add extra yummies, use ½ cup measurements of any of these:

- Chocolate chips
- Chopped nuts
- Coconut
- Berries

My favorite is adding ¼ cup miniature chocolate chips and ¼ cup pecans (total ½ cup)

Super Easy Vanilla Ice Cream II

2 cups heavy cream
14 oz. can sweetened condensed milk
2 teaspoons vanilla extract
¼ teaspoon salt

Beat cream until peaks form. Stir together condensed milk, vanilla and salt. Fold in cream. Pour into ice cream maker for 20 to 30 minutes.

Big Bend National Park in Southwest Texas

Chapter Eight
This and That

While not a staple at mealtime, there are several things that make meals or snack times special. Whether it's lemonade in the summer, frozen hot chocolate for a weekend treat, or Sangria for a summertime cookout, beverages can set the tone for any gathering. In the wintertime, especially at Christmas, I like to make hot apple cider to warm up those cold mornings. My children always loved to have either homemade hot chocolate or hot apple cider Christmas morning as they opened presents and waited for the call to breakfast.

Sauces, like the fudge dessert sauce, make plain vanilla ice cream or pound cake rise to another level. Candies like Mom's cocoa fudge or my version of Fantasy Fudge make Christmas memories.

One of my dearest Christmas memories is making candied pecans. When I lived in Mineola, I had a huge commercial kitchen with a central steel island. There was room in that kitchen for five or six adults to work together to cook a meal. The commercial dishwasher, for which I grieve to this day, would run a load of double stacked dishes, washing and sanitizing, in about 90 seconds. We could eat a full Thanksgiving or Christmas dinner and have all the dishes done and put away by the time everyone had rested sufficiently to start the rounds of desserts. Oh, those were the days.

One Christmas, as usual, I had overcommitted to many friends and neighbors regarding supplying cheese balls and candied pecans for their holiday get togethers. So, in typical fashion, everyone at my house had to join in and help meet our holiday goals. Byron went to the grocery store about ten times, my daughter Raychal organized the parchment paper and started laying out the ingredients, my mother-in-law and father-in-law ran to the Pecan House for MANY pounds of nuts. I felt like a conductor at the symphony. My family is a well-oiled machine.

I stood at the stove for hours making batch after batch of nuts and my family separated them on the parchment paper; packed those that had cooled, and started delivering them. We handled making the cheese balls in the same assembly line manner and finished about ten of them in record time. What would have taken me several days to handle on my own was accomplished in an afternoon filled with laughter, cooperation, and believe it or not, FUN. Several years later, my mother-in-law, Billie, turned to me and said, "remember when you had all those orders for cheese balls and candied pecans? We had so much fun together, didn't we?" Those are the memories that stay with you. Spending quality time with family, helping one another, and enjoying the moment.

Recently, my granddaughter, Ali, came to spend a few days after Thanksgiving. She and I worked together to make cinnamon ornaments, bake them and use them to decorate the Christmas tree and throughout the house. The dough was messy but smelled like the holidays. Before baking the ornament, we used a straw to make a hole in the top for the ribbon used to hang them. I used the straw only a couple of times before I mentioned that I couldn't get the dough out of the straw and making the holes was not working well.

With 11-year old logic, Ali picked up the straw and blew into the other side to remove the dough. She didn't say a word, simply laid the straw down and went back to the ornaments she was working on. Being the best possible Grammy, I bragged on her for hours to anyone who would listen.

Baking the ornaments at a lower temperature for 2 hours at 200 degrees, made the whole house smell like cinnamon. All anyone would want is to take a bite of one of those ornaments but since they contained glue, it would not be a wise decision.

The "This and That" chapter is a compilation of little touches that can make a difference to your friends or family. Another great example is making homemade butter. It is like a great experiment in how to separate liquids and solids. As fun as science can be, the taste of freshly made butter is the real reason you'd want to try it. The process isn't hard but does take some time. The results are an amazing butter flavor and the salt can be completely controlled or left out (if you are going to use it for baking, leave it out). Take the time to look through these recipes to see how you might use one or more to show your friends and family how much you care.

Cinnamon Ornaments

*(looks like dark gingerbread, **but not to be eaten!**)*

2/3 cup apple sauce
4 oz. Cinnamon
2 tablespoons all-purpose glue
1 straw
Parchment paper

Mix apple sauce, cinnamon, and glue until a uniform color and consistency. Knead mixture it forms a smooth dough.

Roll into a circle ¼" thick. Using cookie cutters, press cutter firmly into dough and remove ornament. Using a straw, poke a hole through the top of the ornament and place on parchment paper lined baking sheet.

Either allow to dry naturally for several days or (*if you are like me and too impatient to wait that long*) put the baking sheet in the oven at 200 F for 2-3 hours. They will be ready when they are firm and fragrant.

Thread a ribbon through the hole and hang them on your Christmas tree and around the house. They smell wonderful! This is a fun craft you can share with family and friends.

Lula May's Lemonade

Lula May Mobley was my Great-Grandmother who lived in McKinney, Texas. She was the picture of a southern lady and I never heard her utter a strong word or raise her voice. She was a widow by the time I knew her. Going to her house almost always was a weekend adventure. My mother would get up super early on Saturday morning and drive to McKinney to see her Granny. I would always beg to stay the night and Daddy would have to come on Sunday afternoon to take me home. Granny had a lovely old home and had a nice lady who helped her keep the house, cook and clean. Many days I would sit on the kitchen stool and watch one, or both of them, make Southern meals that appeared effortless.

Summertime in McKinney meant sitting on the screened in porch and sipping this lemonade. A simple recipe but made more special by Granny's preparation method. She insisted that tea or lemonade was always better sweetened with sugar syrup (simple syrup) as opposed to adding granulated sugar that might float to the bottom of the glass or pitcher. I drank hundreds of glasses of lemonade and iced tea on that porch. Every time I make lemonade, I think of her sitting in her wooden rocker, hands folded until she reached for her glass of lemonade. We sat on the porch and solved the world's problems and talked about everything. Her perspective was so simple and her manner so kind. Make lemonade for someone you love; they will remember that you did.

1 cup sugar
1 cup water
10 lemons, cut in half (should result in 1 ½ cups lemon juice)
4 cups cold water

Bring 1 cup sugar and 1 cup water to a boil. Continue until all the sugar dissolves. Remove from heat and cool completely. The result will be simple syrup, or as it is known in the south, sugar syrup.

Put a small strainer over a pint measuring cup. Cut 10 lemons in half and squeeze out 1 ½ cups of juice. Combine lemon juice, sugar syrup and 4 cups cold water.

Taste and if still too tart, add more water but no more than 1 cup. Thinly slice 2 lemons and stir into lemonade pitcher. Chill in the refrigerator for at least 30 minutes or until you are ready to serve.

Best served in tall glasses, poured over lots of ice. Refreshing summertime drink.

Cherry Limeade

3 cups water
1 cup fresh lime juice
1 cup sugar
¾ cup maraschino cherry juice
4 cups lemon-lime flavored carbonated beverage, chilled
Garnish with lime slices, maraschino cherries, fresh mint sprigs

1. In a large pitcher, combine water, lime juice, sugar, and maraschino cherry juice. Stir until sugar dissolves. Chill until ready to serve.

2. Slowly add lemon-lime-flavored carbonated beverage to pitcher, stirring gently to combine. Serve over ice and garnish with lime slices, cherries and fresh mint.

3. This is delightful poured into a tall glass while you sit on the porch and visit with friends. On a tough day, I like to pour about half of the mixture into the ice cream machine, add ¼ cup of vodka and make adult cherry limeade slushes.

Frozen Hot Chocolate

½ cup of chocolate syrup
1 cup whole milk
½ teaspoon vanilla extract
3 cups ice cubes
Garnish with whipped topping and chocolate shavings

Combine chocolate syrup, milk, vanilla and ice in a blender and blend until smooth. Pour into glasses and garnish with a dollop of whipped cream and a sprinkle of chocolate shavings.

For a little variety:

Mexican Frozen Hot Chocolate – add ¼ teaspoon cinnamon

Peppermint Frozen Hot Chocolate – replace vanilla extract with peppermint extract and garnish with a candy cane.

Hot Apple Cider

½ gallon apple cider
2 pints Ginger Ale
16 whole cloves
3 cinnamon sticks
¼ to 1/3 cup red hots

Mix all ingredients in a large pot over medium heat until the red hots are melted. Serve hot. This is a family favorite Christmas morning.

Texas Sunset

1 fifth Champagne
1-quart Ginger ale
1-quart orange juice
1 cup brandy
Crushed Ice

    Combine all ingredients and serve over crushed ice.

Easy White Sangria

1 large orange
1 large lemon
½ cup sugar
2 bottles (750ML) white burgundy or chardonnay wine
1 bottle (quart) sparkling water
1 cup vodka

    Slice the orange and lemon in very thin slices. Remove any seeds. Place in a bowl and add sugar, crush together slightly. Transfer the mixture to a clean pitcher, pour wine over fruit and chill for several hours. Strain and add sparkling water and vodka right before serving.

    Serve over ice and garnish with more fruit.

Mango Bellini's

16 oz. bag frozen mango chunks, thawed
6 tablespoons powdered sugar ½ cup water plus 2 tablespoons of water
one 750ML bottle Champagne or sparkling wine, chilled
Garnish with thin slices of mango or a sprig of mint

Process mango, sugar, and ½ cup plus 2 tablespoons water in a blender for 30 second to 1 minute or until smooth, stopping to scrape down sides of blender. Pour mixture through a wire mesh strainer into a medium bowl, discard solids. Cover and chill until ready to serve.

Spoon 3 tablespoons mango puree into each of 6 champagne flutes. Fill with Champagne; gently stir. Garnish with mango or a sprig of fresh mint. Serve cold.

Hot Fudge Sauce

1 cup semi-sweet chocolate chips
14 oz. can sweetened condensed milk
2 tablespoons butter
2 tablespoons water
1 teaspoon vanilla extract

Melt chocolate chips with sweetened condensed milk, butter, and water in a medium saucepan over medium heat. Beat smooth with a wire whisk then stir in vanilla.

Serve warm over ice cream or as a fruit dipping sauce. Great drizzled over pound cake with whipped cream. Store leftovers in a lidded mason jar in the refrigerator. To reheat, combine the desired amount of sauce with a small amount of water in a small saucepan. Stir constantly over low heat until heated through.

Pecan Honey Butter

My kids loved when I made homemade biscuits with this honey butter. Their dad would fry eggs and ham while the biscuits baked. - This was a Sunday morning favorite!

½ cup butter, softened
½ cup finely chopped toasted pecans
2 tablespoons honey

Stir together the softened butter, toasted pecans, and honey. Mix until completely combined and put in a small jar or decorative bowl. Store in refrigerator up to 1 week or freeze up to 1 month.

Cranberry, Walnut and Orange Butter

½ cup butter
1/3 cup toasted walnuts, chopped
¼ cup dried cranberries, chopped
1 teaspoon orange zest

Stir together the softened butter, toasted walnuts, dried cranberries and orange zest until fully combined. Put in a small container and refrigerate at least 30 minutes prior to serving or roll in wax paper to make a log to slice.

Cherry Honey Butter

1/3 cup dried cranberries or dried cherries
2 teaspoons orange zest
¼ cup honey
1/8 teaspoon salt
1 cup butter

Beat all ingredients and refrigerate at least 4 hours prior to serving.

Lemon Chive Butter

½ cup butter
¼ cup chopped chives
1 teaspoon lemon zest
¼ teaspoon pepper

Add softened butter, chopped chives, lemon zest and pepper to a small mixing bowl and stir to combine. Put in a small container and refrigerate at least 30 minutes prior to serving or roll in wax paper to make a log to slice. Put a pat of this butter on top of your steak and allow to melt into the meat.

Granny's Homemade Butter

2 cups heavy cream, cold
Cheesecloth
Optional: ½ teaspoon of salt
Using a stand mixer, whisk cream on high speed until pale yellow or approximately 8 to 10 minutes. *Optional: Add salt after 5 minutes of whisking.*

While cream mixes, place 3 layers of cheesecloth in a strainer over a large mixing bowl.

The cream will separate into liquid and solid. Transfer the solids to the layered cheesecloth, gathering to form a ball and squeeze out any remaining liquid. Rinse under cold water and pat with paper towels until dry. Shape into a log, using wax paper or parchment to roll.

Fresh butter will last up to 2 weeks if refrigerated. This recipe makes approximately ¾ cup or roughly the equivalent of 1 ½ sticks of butter

Cranberry Sauce

1 bag fresh cranberries
¼ cup orange juice
¼ cup water
¾ cups sugar
Orange zest (half orange)
OPTIONAL: *1 large jalapeno*

Add all ingredients to a medium saucepan and bring to a boil, stirring occasionally until cranberries start to burst. Make sure at least half of the cranberries burst—should take approximately 15 minutes. Put in a nice dish or mold and refrigerate until ready to serve.

Optional: *Sometimes I mince a jalapeno, seeds removed, and stir it in when I add the other ingredients to the saucepan. This is particularly tasty on what I call a "Thanksgiving in my mouth" sandwich. I take a fresh sandwich roll, spread a thin layer of butter on both sides of the roll, stuff turkey or ham in, followed by dressing, gravy, and cranberry sauce. I put this under the broiler until heated throughout This is absolutely my favorite sandwich.*

Caramel Pecan Sauce

1 cup packed brown sugar
1 cup granulated sugar
1/8 cup flour
1 cup water
4 tablespoons butter
1 tablespoon vanilla
1 cup chopped pecans

Combine sugars, flour, and water in a small saucepan. Boil 15 minutes or until mixture is slightly thick. Stir in butter, vanilla and pecans. Serve over ice cream or pound cake slices.

Pralines

1 ½ cups sugar
¾ cup packed light brown sugar
Dash of salt
1/2 cup whole milk
6 tablespoons butter
1 ½ cups pecans
1 tablespoon vanilla (or 1 teaspoon vanilla and 1 teaspoon bourbon or brandy)

    Combine all ingredients and bring to a boil until candy reaches soft ball stage or 238 to 240 degrees, stirring constantly. Remove pan from heat and using a wooden spoon, beat the mixture until it thickens and becomes creamy. Spoon onto buttered parchment paper and allow to cool completely before serving.

Candied Pecans

¼ cup sugar
1 tablespoon butter
1 tablespoon water
¼ teaspoon cinnamon
Dash salt
1 cup pecan halves

    Spray a 10" cast iron skillet with non-stick cooking spray. Combine all ingredients except pecans and cook over medium heat for 5 minutes. Add pecans and cook for an additional 5 minutes or until sugar butter mixture is no longer runny, and pecans start to brown. Pour onto a piece of parchment paper, separating the pecans as you spread them out to cool.

Chipotle Pecans

4 tablespoons butter
4 cups pecan halves
1 tablespoon brown sugar; packed
1 teaspoon cinnamon
½ teaspoon chipotle powder
¼ teaspoon cumin
Salt to taste

Preheat oven to 350 degrees. Line a baking sheet with parchment paper and set aside,

Melt the butter in a skillet on low heat. Add pecans and stir until they are covered in butter. Add the brown sugar, cinnamon, chipotle powder and cumin and stir to coat pecans. Spread the pecans on the prepared baking sheet and place in the oven for 15 minutes. Salt to taste when they come out of the oven.

These are a great snack for happy hours or during the holidays when there are visitors. Be careful, though, as they are habit forming and you will finish off several hands full before you realize you are still eating them.

Mom's Cocoa Fudge

(The recipe yields about 24 squares.)

2/3 cup cocoa
3 cups sugar
1/8 teaspoon salt
1 ½ tablespoons light corn syrup
1 ½ cups milk
4 ½ tablespoons butter
¾ teaspoon vanilla
½ cup chopped nuts

    Combine cocoa with sugar, salt and syrup. Cook to 232 degrees (This is a hard fudge which needs the crystallization achieved at this temperature) or until a small amount of the mixture forms a soft ball when dropped in cold water. Stir several times during the cooking process, to prevent sticking. Remove from heat, drop in butter. Cool to lukewarm (110 degrees), add vanilla and beat until mixture thickens and loses the shiny appearance. Turn into a buttered 8" x 8" square baking pan. Cut into 1 ½" squares when completely cooled.

Old Fashioned Fantasy Fudge

(Yields 3 pounds.)

3 cups sugar
¾ cup butter
2/3 cup Evaporated Milk
12 oz. package semi-sweet chocolate morsels
7 oz. jar marshmallow crème
1 cup chopped nuts
1 teaspoon vanilla
Up to a cup of Walnut halves for decoration

Combine sugar, butter and evaporated milk in a 2 ½ or 3 quart heavy gauge saucepan. Bring to full rolling boil, stirring constantly. Continue boiling 5 minutes over medium heat or until candy thermometer reaches 234F; ***stir constantly to prevent scorching***. Remove from heat. Stir in semi-sweet chocolate morsels until melted. Add marshmallow crème, nuts, and vanilla; beat until well blended. Pour into greased 13x9" baking pan. Top with walnut halves pressed into the fudge. Let cool at room temperature and wait fifteen minutes, then cut into squares.

Stocking your kitchen – spice rack gives quick access without taking much counterspace

Chapter Nine
Stocking Your Kitchen

Whether you are setting up your kitchen for the first time or just want to make sure you have the basics, this section will help outline what is needed for a fully functioning kitchen. When I was growing up, my mother's kitchen was overflowing with multiple mixing bowls, skillets, and every kitchen gadget that came on the market. Many of which she seldom used. She was constantly adding to her collection of items until we were all afraid to open a cabinet or drawer. When cooking in her kitchen, there was never a substitution for a particular pan or utensil, just had to look around a little bit. What I didn't realize at the time was that hers was an accumulation of over 35 years of collecting. But, for most of us, the reality is to start slowly, on a budget, and realize that we might need to weigh whether an item is a necessity.

This section focuses on how to set up and stock a kitchen that will enable you to have all the basics, make substitutions for specialty items, and prioritize adding additional cookware, serving dishes, utensils, etc. Building out the perfect kitchen is not an absolute formula as each of us has specific ideas about wants, needs, and nice to haves. While every individual could go through a process to determine his or her needs in the kitchen, there are some minimum requirements every kitchen should have stocked.

When Byron and I married, we moved into a one-bedroom apartment with a pretty small kitchen. Each of us brought some items to outfit the kitchen but there were huge gaps in pans, utensils, and small appliances. It seemed like we each brought about the same things. Thinking about my mother's (or his mother's) kitchen, then looking at mine, and realizing we had a strict budget, I needed a plan of action. I will tell you that I had no idea where to start. What did I need first? What could I wait to get later?

So, I sat down in the living room with a pen, paper and a copy of the Betty Crocker cookbook my mother had given me. I looked at recipes I had tried, wanted to try, or thought Byron would like. Then I started putting together a list of pans, utensils, small appliances and ingredients needed for those recipes. After working for a couple of hours, I stopped gathering recipes and started looking through my notes for items that were repeated multiple times. From that effort, I put together a list of "must have", "nice to have", and "someday I will have".

Although it was a tedious undertaking, I quickly decided on the few items I needed immediately. I also found myself sharing my process with friends, colleagues, and family members who were moving out on their own or getting married. My suggestion is to start with the basics everyone needs, then move slowly through the list of "nice to have(s)", based on your and/or your significant other's preferences. You will be surprised how quickly, using this method, that you'll get to the "someday I'll have" items.

Here are my suggestions for fully stocking your kitchen to prepare most of your favorite meals. There are some variations you can use to save time or to improve freshness

Dry Goods:

Flour –all purpose, whole wheat and self-rising (already includes baking powder, salt, etc.)

Sugar –white, brown, and confectioner's (powdered)

Rolled Oats

Rice –long-grain, white and brown

Cornmeal

Baking Soda –used when the recipe features an acidic ingredient like buttermilk, cream of tartar, or citrus juice

Baking Powder –used when the recipe does not have one of the acidic ingredients listed above

Cornstarch

Cream of tartar

Cocoa Powder –unsweetened

Chocolate –chips and/or bars

Dry Beans –black, cannellini, navy, kidney, garbanzo, and/or pinto

Pasta –long shapes, small shapes, couscous, spaghetti

Dried Breadcrumbs

Coffee

Tea

Oils, Vinegars, and Sauces:

Oils –vegetable or canola, extra virgin olive, and non-stick cooking spray

Vinegars –apple cider, red wine, white and clear.

Vanilla Extract –get the pure extract and stay away from imitation vanilla

Almond Extract

Soy Sauce

Worcestershire Sauce

Honey

Maple Syrup

Mustard –yellow and Dijon or brown

Mayonnaise

Herbs and Spices:

Sea Salt –available in many varieties and in large or fine grains and ranges in color from white to pink or brown. Best used at the end of cooking to season food.

Whole Peppercorns –or coarse ground, I prefer to grind my own for the freshest results.

Bay Leaves –lends a savory or spicy touch to pickles, soups, stews, meat or casseroles

Basil –fresh green or purple leaves or dried and/or crushed. Adds a sweet flavor with hints of mint pepper and cloves. Best used for tomato sauce, pesto, chicken, meat, zucchini, summer squashes. Great on pizza.

Oregano –available as fresh leaves, dried and/or crushed or ground. Slightly bitter but savory flavor used for tomato dishes, chicken, pork, and vegetables.

Thyme –available as fresh leaves or dried and/or crushed. Earthy, spicy flavor that partners well for meat, poultry, beans soups or stews.

Cumin -available as seed or ground. Earthy, aromatic flavor used for beans, chili, pork, chicken, soups or stews.

Crushed Red Pepper -spicy flavor which can be used for soups, stews, sauces, or sprinkled on meats, vegetables, or pizza.

Cayenne Pepper -available ground. Spicy addition to chili, soups, sauces, beans, poultry, meat or seafood.

Paprika -available ground. Mild to hot sweet flavor addition to poultry, shellfish, meat or vegetables.

Cinnamon -available as sticks or ground. Sweet flavor addition to baked goods, fruit desserts, and warm beverages.

Chili Powder -available ground. Spicy flavor addition to chili, meats, or beans.

Garlic powder -savory flavor to add to soups, stews, meats or vegetables.

Cocoa Powder -available ground. Adds chocolate flavor to desserts or richness to savory sauces or soups.

Bouillon cubes – keep both beef and chicken on hand.

Canned Goods:

Chicken Broth

Tomatoes -paste, diced, crushed, and sauce

Beans -pinto, black, kidney, white, garbanzo (aka chickpea)

Vegetables -hominy, corn, green beans, carrots (alternately buy fresh or freeze dried)

Tuna

Pumpkin Puree

Pasta Sauces -both tomato and cream based

Milk -coconut, sweetened condensed, evaporated

Refrigerator:

Milk –dairy or non-dairy

Eggs

Butter –salted and unsalted (if you can only choose one, choose unsalted

Meat –bacon and ham as staples and any additional meats you intend to cook

Plain Yogurt

Cheese –parmesan, cheddar, Monterey jack

Fresh Produce –avocados, carrots, celery, tomatoes (cherry, regular), leafy greens, lettuce, onions, lemons/limes, and apples

Jelly –jam or preserves

Freezer:

Fruit –blueberries, strawberries, peaches and/or cherries

Vegetables –chopped broccoli, corn, and/or okra

Meats –ground beef, beef, ground turkey or Italian Sausage, boneless/skinless chicken breasts, and/or bacon

Bread –dough, pie or puff pastry

Vanilla Ice Cream

Measuring Tools:

Liquid measuring cups – I suggest at least a 1 cup and a 4-cup size. Although liquid measuring cups vary in size from a 1 cup to 8 cup size, it is most important to have a 1 cup liquid measuring cup to start. If you could only choose one, choose the 1 cup. If you can have two, choose a 1 cup and a large, probably 4 cup to mix small batters or combine several liquid measures.

Set of Dry measuring cups – on the other hand, dry measuring cups should be purchased in a set that includes at least ¼ cup, 1/3 cup, ½ cup, and 1 cup sizes. Invest in a good set of sturdy measuring cups as you will use these daily.

Set of Measuring Spoons – another tool that you will likely use often are measuring spoons. Most spoon sets include ¼-teaspoon, ½-teaspoon, 1-teaspoon and 1-tablespoon. So, spend a little extra to make sure you have a good set of spoons that will stand up to constant use. Measuring spoons are used to measure both liquid and dry ingredients in smaller increments.

Bakeware:

Two or three **9" x 1-1/2" round baking pans** (for cakes)

One **half sheet pan**

One **quarter sheet pan**

One **13" x 9" baking pan** (cakes/casseroles)

One **15" x 10" baking pan (jelly roll pan)** – this item can be used for jelly rolls, oven roasting vegetables or bacon, sheets of brownies or bar cookies, and can be used to replace a cookie sheet if you can only afford one or the other. In that case, opt for the jelly roll pan as it will serve so many purposes in the kitchen.

One **9" pie plate**

One 12 cup **muffin pan** (standard size)

Two **9" x 5" loaf pans** and/or two **8" x 4" loaf pans** (in a new kitchen, opt for the 8" x 4" as most recipes call for that size)

One **8" x 8" square baking pan**

One **Bundt pan** or **tube pan** (sometimes called an angel food pan)

Cookware:

One **Dutch Oven (5 qt.)**

One **8" or 9" sauté/omelet pan**

One **8" cast iron skillet**

One **10" skillet**

One **1 qt. saucepan**

One **2 qt. saucepan** (as soon as possible, add a shallow roasting pan with rack)

Knives:

One of the most important cooking tools, knives are probably the highest investment in your kitchen. Many dependable brands provide a knife set with storage block that includes at least the following:

Chef's knife (8" or 10" blade) – used for mincing or chopping.

Santoku (6-1/2" or 7") – used for mincing, chopping, and slicing.

Carving (8" or 10") – used for slicing meats

Serrated or Bread (8") – used for slicing breads, cakes or vegetables such as tomatoes.

Utility (6") – used for slicing smaller foods

Boning (5" or 6") – used for removing meat and separating from bone.

Paring (3" or 4") – used for peeling, mincing or slicing smaller foods.

Kitchen Shears – used for herbs, cutting chicken, or trimming pastry for pies.

Sharpening Steel – used to keep knives sharp or smooth out blades.

Organize and measure your ingredients before you begin

Chapter Ten
Meal Preparation

Kitchen hints and tips to make life easier:

1. When uniform pieces of meat are required, place the meat in the freezer for a minimum of 20 minutes to easier cut into cubes or slices.
2. Don't bother peeling garlic if you intend to smash it for sauces, etc. Simply cut off the root, smash the garlic with the flat side of a knife blade and remove any loose peel.
3. You can peel ginger with a spoon to ensure you don't lose all that extra ginger that remains when trimming with a knife.
4. Use unscented floss to through soft items such as cheese, cakes or when making cinnamon rolls.
5. Egg shells are best for fishing out bits of eggshell. Why? Because they're sharp and cut through the egg.
6. Keep butter in the freezer and then grate it for baking and pastries. It mixes into the flour easier and melts quicker.
7. Hard boiled eggs peel easiest if you add some baking soda to the pot of water and then place into cold water afterwards.
8. Freeze bananas without skins for smoothies, muffins or other recipes.
9. Spray measuring cups with non-stick cooking spray prior to measuring sticky items like syrups, honey, molasses, etc. Doing so will enable you use the entire ingredient for the recipe and helps with cleanup.
10. Peel potatoes after you've cooked them and soaked them in cold water for a short time. The skins will come off quickly.
11. Where recipes in this book call for sifted flour, measure then sift to get the right volume. Sifting gives a lighter –more fluffy– result, so for best effect, don't skip this step.

Measuring Correctly is the Key to Success:

Liquids: most liquid measuring cups are either glass or plastic and have a pour spout to assist in making sure you get all the liquid ingredients required for the recipe. Many also have a handle which makes it easier to hold as you pour. Always place the measuring cup on a level surface and try to view at eye level. Try not to lift the cup as doing so will impact measurement. (Note: prior to measuring sticky ingredients like syrups or hones, spray the measuring cup with non-stick cooking spray to avoid sticking and to ensure you get all the ingredient needed for a specific recipe).

Shortening: when measuring shortening, press into dry measuring cup with a spatula to be sure there is a solid measurement and no air pockets. Blocks or sticks of shortening can be measured like butter.

Dry ingredients or yogurt: dry measuring cups are used to measure ingredients such as flour, sugar, or shortening. The dry measuring cups are used to measure ingredients such as flour, sugar or shortening. The dry measuring cups have a flat surface for ease in leveling to ensure accurate measurement. Spoon the ingredient into a dry measuring cup then level the top by sweeping a metal spatula or the flat side of a knife across the top. It is better to over fill, then level, to ensure accurate measurement.

Butter: the wrappers for sticks of butter come with markings, in tablespoon increments, for ease in measurement. Most also include the ¼ cup (4 tablespoons or a half-stick) or ½ cup (8 tablespoons or a full stick).

Brown Sugar: unless otherwise noted in a recipe, brown sugar should always be firmly packed into a measuring cup and leveled as other dry ingredients.

Measurement conversions:

1/8 cup = 2 tablespoons

¼ cup = 4 tablespoons

1/3 cup = 5 tablespoons

½ cup = 8 tablespoons

2/3 cup = 10 tablespoons

¾ cup = 12 tablespoons

1 cup = 16 tablespoons

Other Handy serving facts:

12 quarts of punch will fill 96 punch cups

1 gallon of punch serves 20

1 gallon of ice cream serves 30 scoops

A 4 lb. hen yields 4 cups diced chicken

Typical Restaurant size servings you can expect from round pan dishes:

Pies:

10" pie will serve 8

9" pie will serve 7

8" pie will serve 6

Cakes:

8" round layer cake will serve 16

14" round layer cake will serve 25

18" x 25" sheet cake will serve 48

Common Cooking Techniques

Baking – foods are put on or in a pan and baked in an oven until thoroughly and evenly cooked. Breads, pies, and cookies are all baked in a moderate oven.

Biscuits – When baking biscuits, judge by smell and color than strictly following a suggested time limit. They will begin to smell "nutty" when they are at peak. Also, the bottoms will be golden and the tops just start showing color.

Frying – foods are cooked in hot oil. Typically, depending on the item being fried, the skillet or pan should contain a ½" to 1" of hot oil. Fry, uncovered, until the food is cooked through.

Sautéing – foods are cooked in a very small amount of hot oil in a skillet or sauté pan. Vegetables are cooked quickly and should be stirred frequently.

Braising – foods, like meat, are browned, in a Dutch oven, in a small amount of oil and then some liquid is added. The pot is then covered, and the items allowed to simmer until cooked.

Common Cuts

Dicing or cubing vegetables – use a Utility Knife or Santoku to trim each side of the vegetable to square it. Cut into evenly sized strips or cubes. The narrower the strip, the smaller the pieces will be. Dicing cuts are typically 1/8" to ¼" and cubes are general 1/2" to 1". Arrange strips and cut into desired size pieces. Keeping pieces uniform in size aids in even cooking.

Mincing or Chopping – holding the handle of a Chef's Knife or Santoku with one hand, blade downward, rest the fingers of your other hand on the top of the blade, near the tip. This will help guide your strokes. Using the handle to apply pressure, move the knife up and across the food with a rocking motion, moving back and forth until the pieces of food are the size desired. When minced, pieces are generally no larger than 18" and when chopped, ¼" to 1/2".

Recipe Index

Chapter Three – Let's Get Started

Appetizers

Baby Girl's Cheese Ball	21
Baked Brie or Camembert	32
Baked Chicken Wings	30
Brie en Croute	31
Cheese and Honey Fondue	33
Cheese Crisp Cookies	24
Creamy Dreamy Queso	25
Four Layer Crab Dip	23
Guacamole	26
Jam & Brie Tarts	32
Lazy Day Guacamole	26
Love Dip	19
Mexi-Mushrooms	29
Pico de Gallo	27
Quick Salsa	28
Shrimp Dip	18
Tomatillo Salsa	28
White Queso	25

Soups

30-Minute Tortilla Soup	38
Corn and Crab Bisque	35
Creole Gumbo	40
Hearty Beef Stew	36
Pumpkin Soup	34
Strawberry Soup	34

Salads

Bebe's Favorite Chicken Salad	41
Blue Cheese Dressing	42
Broccoli Salad	44
Cole Slaw	45
Cranberry Marshmallow Salad	42
Cucumbers with Sour Cream Dressing	45
Fruited Chicken Salad	46
Ham and Blue Cheese Pasta Salad	41
Hot Bacon Dressing	43
Orange Vinaigrette	48
Pistachio Fluff	47
Potato Salad	47
Spicy Lime Vinaigrette	49
Spinach Apricot Salad	44
Spinach Salad with Hot Bacon Dressing	43
Tomato, Avocado and Cucumber Salad	46
Tuna Salad	48

Chapter Four – Bread and Breakfast

Bread

Bebe's Blueberry Biscuits	60
Bebe's Quick Biscuits	57
Beer Biscuits	58
Beer Bread	88
Biscuit Cinnamon Rolls	71
Breakfast Sweet Bread	73
Broccoli Cornbread	84

Cheddar Biscuits	61
Cornbread	81
Cranberry Artisan Bread	78
Cranberry Orange (or Cherry Almond) Scones	64
Easy Peasy Blueberry Muffins	66
Garlic Cheese Toast	88
Gingerbread Muffins	69
Harvest Apple Bread	75
Jalapeno Cornbread Muffins	85
Just Peachy Muffins	67
Lemon Tea Bread	74
Mamaw's Biscuits	54
Maple Ginger Glaze	65
Mexican Cornbread	86
Nanner Bread	76
Never Fail Popovers	87
Pecan Pie Muffins	68
Pretty as a Peach Scones	63
Pumpkin Scones with Maple Ginger Glaze	65
Sausage Gravy for Biscuits	58
Small Soda Bread	79
Strawberries in a Biscuit	61
Sugar Syrup for Biscuits	55
Super Small Super Good Scones	62
Sweet Cornbread Cake	84
Sweet Potato Apple Walnut Muffins	72
Tomato Bread	83
Tropical Banana Bread	77
Vanilla Bean Scones	64
Yeast Rolls	80

Breakfast

Apple Cinnamon Baked Oatmeal	94
Blueberry Croissant Breakfast Puff	93
Breakfast Casserole	98
Breakfast Sausage	102
Chocolate Banana Oatmeal Cups	95
Easy Breakfast Potatoes	103
Grand Marnier French Toast	89
Granny's Pancakes	90
Ham and Swiss Strata	101
Hearty Sweet Potato Hash	99
Honey Baked Pancake	91
Max's Green Chile Casserole	97
Mediterranean Quiche	100
Night Before Christmas French Toast	89
Oven Omelet	96
Weekend Baked Apple Pancake	92

Chapter Five–The Main Event

Beef

Chicken Fried Steak with Gravy	108
Bowl of Red aka Texas Chili	110
Tacos al Carbon	111
Baked Ziti	112
Mom's Goulash	113
Beef Empanadas	114
Granny's Perfect Pot Roast	116
Beef Tenderloin with Champagne Mustard Sauce	117

| Beef Stroganoff | 118 |

Chicken

Apricot Chicken	119
Chicken Alfredo Casserole	122
Chicken and Dumplings	124
Chicken Pecan Fettuccine	126
Chicken Piccata	132
Chicken Pot Pie	123
Chicken Skewers with Thai Peanut Sauce	125
Crock Pot Tetrazzini	129
Garlic and Citrus Roasted Chicken	131
King Ranch Chicken	128
Sharon's Chicken Tacos/Flautas	120
Sour Cream Chicken Enchiladas	127
Tequila-Lime Chicken Drumsticks	130
White Chicken Chili	121

Pork

Baked Ham with Honey-Mustard Sauce	135
Grilled Pork Chops with Wine Sauce	134
Ham, Asparagus & Gruyere Quiche	137
Parmesan Pork Chops	135
Slow Cooker Ribs	133
Southern Baked Ham	138

Seafood

Jumbo Crab Cakes with Chive Aioli	139
Mom's Tuna Casserole	138
Shrimp Creole	140

Vegetarian

Cheese Enchiladas with Red Sauce	141

Chapter Six – On the Side

Vegetables

Baked Beans	166
Baked Mashed Potatoes	169
Black-Eyed Peas	151
Byron's Collard Greens	165
Byron's Cream Peas	156
Cheesy Grits Casserole	150
Corn Pudding	152
Cornbread Dressing	160
Fried Green Tomatoes	164
Fried Okra	148
Gravy for Dressing	161
Mexican Rice	166
Nanny's Hominy Casserole	164
Okra and Tomatoes	147
Pop's Pinto Beans & Refried Leftover Beans	157
Refried Beans	165
Roasted Asparagus	155
Roasted Brussel Sprouts	167
Roasted Harvest Vegetables	161
Roasted Parmesan Green Beans	153
Scalloped Potatoes	149
Southern Fried Cabbage	158
Southern Sweet Potato Casserole	168
Squash Casserole	159
Texas Tomato Pie	163
Tomato Tart (like pizza)	162

Chapter Seven - Perfect Endings

Cake

Apple Spice Cake	176
Gingerbread Pound Cake with Lemon Sauce	177
Mom's Coca Cola Cake	174
Peach Cobbler Snack Cake	173
Pineapple Upside Down Cake	178
Texas Tornado Cake	175

Pies

Barb's Chocolate Pie	188
Buttermilk Pie	182
Buttermilk Pie Crust	181
Coconut Cream Pie	187
Pecan Pie	186
Sawdust Pie	183
Sugar Cream Pie	179
Sweet Potato Pecan Pie	184

Cookies

Ali's Peanut Butter Cookies	201
Bebe's Lemon Bars	192
Chocolate Dipped Coconut Macaroons	191
Cranberry White Chocolate Oatmeal Cookies	199
Gingerbread Molasses Cookies	197
Granny Mobley's Sugar Cookies	193
Hello Dolly Squares	189
Pecan Puffs	202
Pecan Tassies	200
Snickerdoodles	196

Texas Cow Chips 198
World's Best Brownies 195

Desserts

Best Dang Blackberry Cobbler 203
Cherry Clafoutis 205
Mom's Chocolate Pudding 206
Banana Pudding 207
Super Easy Vanilla Ice Cream I 208
Super Easy Vanilla Ice Cream II 209

Chapter Eight - This and That

Cinnamon Ornaments (not to be eaten) 213

Beverages

Cherry Limeade 215
Easy White Sangria 217
Frozen Hot Chocolate 216
Hot Apple Cider 216
Lula May's Lemonade 214
Mango Bellini's 218
Texas Sunset 217

Sauces

Caramel Pecan Sauce 221
Cherry Honey Butter 219
Cranberry Sauce 221
Cranberry, Walnut & Orange Butter 219
Granny's Homemade Butter 220
Hot Fudge Sauce 218

Lemon Chive Butter	220
Pecan Honey Butter	219

Candy

Candied Pecans	222
Chipotle Pecans	223
Mom's Cocoa Fudge	224
Old Fashioned Fantasy Fudge	225
Pralines	222

www.ingramcontent.com/pod-product-compliance
Lightning Source LLC
Chambersburg PA
CBHW081228080526
44587CB00022B/3855